Making Word 2010 Work for You

An Editor's Intro to the Tool of the Trade

Hilary Powers

EDITORIAL
FREELANCERS
ASSOCIATION

Editorial Freelancers Association
71 West 23rd Street, 4th Floor
New York, NY 10010
http://www.the-efa.org
Publications Chair: Barbara Magalnick

Editor: Karen Wallace
Proofreader: Rebecca S. Bender
Indexer: Judith Reveal
Cover and Interior Designer: Christine Hunt

The Editorial Freelancers Association (EFA) is a national not-for-profit organization, headquartered in New York City, and run almost entirely by volunteers. Its members, experienced in a wide range of professional skills, live and work in the United States and abroad. EFA was formed in order to develop and implement programs of benefit to professional editorial freelancers and the publishing industry, and to support and advance the interests of both. Members have expertise in a variety of specialties, subject areas, and media; they include abstractors, copyeditors, designers, desktop publishing experts, developmental editors, indexers, manuscript evaluators, picture researchers, project managers, proofreaders, researchers, textbook development editors, translators, and writers.

ISBN 13: 978-1-880407-32-5

Printed in the United States of America

Contents

List of Figures and Tables

Figures

Tables

AUTHOR'S NOTE

Word 2010 has been out for years—and I've been using it from the get-go. So why has this book been so long in reaching the light of day? For years, I believed that virtually everything I knew about Word 2003 had transferred straight into Word 2010 for me, and so what my book said about Word 2003 would work as well for anyone. But bits and pieces have accumulated. There really is more to be said....

This book shares a philosophy (and a fair amount of text) with the original *Making Word Work for You*, but all the specific examples are designed to work with Word 2010.

Introduction: With Your Computer, Not Just on It

Assuming you already know how to edit, you can edit in Word 2010. That is, you can edit in Word 2010 if you know how to get at the files and make changes in them—beyond opening a file, typing and deleting text, and saving, the absolute skill requirement is essentially zero. But you won't like the experience much. You'll probably soon join the ranks of those who maintain that editing on screen is harder than editing on paper, more exposed to error and less conducive to physical health, and generally a bad deal all around.

The problem isn't in the tool, though. It's in its use. If you really want your computer to act like a stack of paper and a set of colored pencils, you can make it do so. Sort of. But if instead you use it for what it is—which requires a different approach to the work and a different set of tricks—editing on screen becomes easier (and faster) than editing on paper, and neither less accurate nor harder on your body. (And, as more and more prospective clients are expecting edits in electronic files, an ability to edit on screen becomes more and more essential to health and happiness.)

The biggest difference between paper editing and on-screen editing is that a straight line is no longer the shortest distance between two points. That is, the steps in the edit are different, and there are more of them, and tasks may happen in a different order from what would work best on paper, but the final effect is that high-quality, medium-level commercial editing—giving a publisher two full read-throughs with substantive overtones and addressing thoughtful queries to the author—can be done at a net rate (considering all the pages and all the time spent on the job) that should come in anywhere between half again and three times as fast as what you can do on paper.

Hard to swallow? Read on….

Where We're Going

A full description of Microsoft Word 2010 and all its uses in all sorts of editing could easily run ten times the size of this little book, so I've had to make a lot of choices about what to present and how to present it. The reader I pictured when deciding whose interests should govern the selection is someone who has fairly substantial experience as a copyeditor of books or journal articles and just enough knowledge of Word 2010 to get a file open and start trying to work by instinct. If all goes well, that reader will find enough solid information about the program here (and more to the point, enough of the mind-set of Word-whacking) to make it feel like a cooperative and friendly tool instead of an interfering and alien environment.

If your experience or interests differ, please bear with me. There's still a lot for you here, but you might want to pick and choose based on this introduction and the subheads in the table of contents, or look things up in the index, rather than reading straight through.

Those who do read from cover to cover will start by getting acquainted with what Word 2010 can do without worrying about the details of how to do it. After all, there's a lot to keep track of about this everything-for-everybody all-purpose tool, and the first and most important thing to know is why you might want to know any of the rest of it.

Then the book follows Word 2010 from its plain-vanilla state—what you get when you load the software and open it for the first time—through more and more active ways to make it stop doing its thing and start doing yours.

Note: Almost everything here addresses ways to modify text rather than ways to make a manuscript look like a finished book. That reflects the state of my knowledge: I know lots about text manipulation and almost nothing about formatting, because in my corner of the editing world, the main thing to know about formatting is how to get rid of it.

Here's a brief outline:

Chapter 1. The Shortest Distance: A Concrete Example: Here I detour to the world of travel to provide a detailed example of the way the mind-set of *using* your computer differs from that of making paper procedures work on screen. This mind-set is what allows me to claim such astonishing speed boosts for real electronic editing.

Chapter 2. Building a Working Environment: What you see on the basic Word 2010 screen (or could see with a few mouse clicks), how it serves you, and what to do if you don't like it.

Chapter 3. Finding Work for Word's Idle Hands: Where Word 2010 hides the settings that make it second-guess what you're doing, how to fix them, and how to use the basic services the program offers, including AutoCorrect, Find and Replace, and the spelling checker.

Chapter 4. Deploying the Custom Features: Where to get hold of the things Word 2010 is built to do but won't volunteer, like keeping track of vocabulary you don't want to use even though it's properly spelled, rearranging the keyboard and ribbon, storing text for quick reuse, and accepting your spoken commands.

Chapter 5. Macros and Templates: Digging into the guts of making Word 2010 do your thing instead of its own—with exercises you can use to get up to speed.

Chapter 6. Domesticating Tracked Changes: How to use the built-in tracking feature smoothly and comfortably, and how to keep its markup simple enough to avoid frightening your authors.

Chapter 7. Coping with Snares and Pitfalls: Where Word's bodies are buried, and how to keep them from rising from their graves and haunting your work.

Chapter 8. Locating Useful Additions: Sources of tools, books, and ongoing advice about Word 2010.

Chapter 9. A Bouquet of Sample Shortcuts: Some macros—mostly easy and easily understood—to start your collection and give you resources to cannibalize for your first adventures in command development.

Chapter 10. Walking Through a Job: The steps involved in a fairly generic nonfiction edit, with notes on ways I use Word 2010 to help in the process.

The rest of this introduction discusses the logic of focusing on Word 2010 and outlines the terminology used in the book.

What Word to Use

This book is built on the assumption that you're using Word 2010, or perhaps some later version that offers many of the same features. For versions preceding Word 2007, *Making Word Work for You*—which remains available—is the book to use. Brand-new Word 2010 users may find it useful to supplement this book by working through Microsoft's tutorial at http://.microsoft.com/en-us/word-help/work-between-new-and-earlier-versions-RZ101816356.aspx?section=1(http://tinyurl.com/Word2010tut). I certainly did. Even if you're not going to accept the Microsoft Way with all its twists and turns, the developers' expectations make a good starting point.

Why focus on Word 2010? It's the playtested version of Word 2007, as Word 2003 was for its predecessor, and it does a lot to moderate Word 2007's take-it-and-lump-it interface. Much of what I recommend here will work in Word 2007, but I'm not sure what won't; I cheerfully bypassed that version. I do know that any attempt to customize the ribbon within Word 2007 is guaranteed not to work—it's one of the main reasons I sat that one out.

Note: The initial release of Word 2007 had some serious problems that were fixed in later service packs from Microsoft; as of this writing, Service Pack 3 is the most recent. So, if you're using Word 2007, make sure it's updated. If you use Word 2010 to open a file saved in Word 2007 and most of the periods have disappeared from the ends of sentences, what you're seeing is the output of an unpatched program.

As I write, the next version—Word 2013—is just going on sale, but *Office Watch* maintains there's no reason to buy it unless you've got a naked computer and no legal way to put Word 2010 on it, and I tend to agree. Word 2013 has a similar ribbon-based user interface, though with more animations, and the write-ups I've read don't make it sound like something editors are apt to feel they have to have, unless clients insist on the web-based document sharing. The default Track Changes function shows only the current final text most of the time; to see what's been done, you need to click the change bar and read text that appears off to one side. You can coax the program to show you all the changes in the old familiar format, but with new, "more modern" colors.... The big innovation is in marketing: Word 2013 is hot-linked to your wallet. That is, it's being pushed as software-as-a-service (where you pay a yearly subscription and get whatever Microsoft is currently offering), and the boxed version includes only one license instead of the two that came with Word 2010.

For Mac users determined to stay under the Apple tree, this book's general philosophy and approach to on-screen editing will be useful, but Word 2011 is a sufficiently different animal that parts of the specific advice may prove difficult to apply. At least Word 2011 has got a version of the VBA macro language used in Word 2010 (unlike the situation with the 2007/2008 release), but it's not perfectly compatible; some of the after-market tools I recommend will work in a Mac environment, but others will not. And even when my advice and suggested tools do work on a Mac, screen locations as well as file locations may differ, and commands may need more adjustment than just substituting Command for Ctrl and Option for Alt.

Many Mac users also have the alternative of loading Parallels or another PC-emulation system and running Word 2010 there. In my admittedly prejudiced view, that's the best course of action if it's available to you. Word just isn't exactly suited to the Mac. It's as though Microsoft were saying, "Oh dear, our basic hammer didn't quite fit in your beautiful toolbox, so we put this nifty hinge behind the head and now it slips right in!" Yah sure, you betchums—but it's now a hammer with a hinge in the handle....

Finding a Common Language

You don't need a lot of jargon to keep up with explanations of things to do with Word 2010. Nonetheless, some terms wind up with meanings you won't see elsewhere, and it's useful to get those down first.

Things

If you've read my pre-2007 book, you'll find that the terminology has changed a bit for this one. The fourth edition of the *Microsoft Manual of Style* took a different view of the what's-that-moving-thing-on-the-screen debate, advising writers to use *cursor* in place of *insertion point*, reviving that pleasantly geeky word. It also recommended using *pointer* in place of *mouse pointer*—which makes sense, given the multiplicity of techniques for moving that symbol around the screen. I'm following Microsoft on these terms here.

Cursor: The place on the screen where the next typed character will appear when you *press* a key; usually shown by a blinking vertical line.

Pointer: The symbol that indicates where the pointing device (mouse, trackball, touchpad, whatever; they all use a *pointer*) is focused; it doesn't blink, and its shape indicates what will happen if you *click* it: usually, make the *cursor* jump to that spot on the screen or activate a *ribbon tab*, an *icon*, or a virtual *button*.

> *Neat pointer trick*: Go to Mouse on the Windows Control Panel and check off "Show location of pointer when I press the CTRL key." Then—when you lose the sneaky thing somewhere on your humongous spread of monitors—you can find it easily, because this setting will put concentric circles around it like ripples around a dropped stone in a pond.
>
> *Note:* The fastest way to the Control Panel is to click Start, then click Control Panel in the right pane. If you have your Control Panel set to Category view, click on Hardware and Sound to get to the Mouse item.

Key: One of the thingies on the keyboard; it makes something happen when you *press* it.

Button:

- *Physical:* One of the thingies on the pointing device; it makes something happen when you push on it.
- *Virtual*: An area on the screen that is designed to resemble a physical *button*; it makes something happen when you *click* it with the pointing device.

Ribbon and Tabs: The band across the top of the screen where Word 2010 puts labeled groups of *icons* for what its developers fondly regard as related functions. You can minimize it and see something that looks like the old Menu bar until you click one of the *tabs*, or just leave it open if you have the screen real estate for it.

Menu and Submenu: The old lists of actions that pre-2007 Word would do for you (File, Edit, View, and so on), and the sets of items that revealed themselves when you *clicked* something on a *menu*. These items are gone from Word 2010, but not forgotten; the same *keys* work to activate their functions. For example, the cascading sequence Insert, Reference, Footnote no longer exists, but the key combination Alt+I, N, N still gets you to the dialog where you can insert or reformat footnotes and endnotes. This book includes still-useful key combinations where appropriate, along with the corresponding *ribbon* locations.

Context Menu: The set of choices that appear when you *right-click* something on the screen; what you see depends on where you *click*, and Word 2010 is fairly good at coming up with a relevant list. The context menus come in handy when you aren't sure what functions are available at a given point, and when you need something too rarely to make it worth hanging on a hot key.

Toolbar: A collection of virtual *buttons* (also called *icons*), each of which performs a specific action when you *click* it. In Word 2010, the only one left is the Quick Access Toolbar, where you can put whatever functions you want access to at all times.

Pilcrow: A paragraph mark—the character Word uses on screen to indicate what's still (from typewriter days) called a "hard carriage return." It looks like this: ¶.

Actions

Press: Activate a *key* on the keyboard, producing a character on the screen or causing some programmed action to take place.

Click: Move the *pointer* to whatever is named and do whatever the pointing device requires to activate it for the indicated purpose—push on a physical *button*, tap on a touchpad, whatever.

Double-click: Move the *pointer* to whatever is named and do whatever the pointing device requires to activate it for the indicated purpose—push on one physical *button* twice, push once on a different physical *button* if you keep one set up for this function, tap a touchpad quickly twice, whatever.

Right-click: Move the *pointer* to whatever is named and do whatever the pointing device requires to activate the pop-up *context menu* of chores you can tell the computer to do at that spot on the screen. The name comes from your basic mouse set up for right-handed use, because you get the effect by pushing on the right-most physical *button*.

Mouse: Move the *pointer* to whatever is named (and usually wait for new information or choices to appear there before you do anything else).

Select: Highlight something on the screen so that you can copy, delete, or otherwise manipulate it.

Key Patterns

Individual key: Indicated by whatever is printed on the face: "Press the A key" means to press that key with no modifiers (as if you were typing the lowercase letter "a").

Simultaneous combinations: "Press Shift+A" means you should press both keys at the same time; in this case, you would type the uppercase letter "A." Other combinations involve Ctrl (usually Command on a Mac, though Macs also make some use of the Ctrl key), Alt (Option on a Mac), or any two or three of these modifiers. ("Press Ctrl+Shift+F9" calls for pressing all three keys together.)

Sequential combinations: "Press Alt+A, C" means you should press Alt and A (that is, lowercase "a") together, release them, and then press C.

Function keys: Numbers preceded by the letter F refer to the labeled keys across the top of the keyboard in their original Microsoft-issue state. If you press one and get different results from those I describe, chances are an add-in has hijacked it. See "Using Templates" in chapter 5 for advice on restoring default behavior for the current session, so you can see if you want to restore it or at least put it where you can find it.

Getting Started

OK. Enough noodling. Time to sit down at the screen and start to play….

Play is the operative word, by the by; I can tell you a lot about the kinds of things Word 2010 does, but I can't begin to cover all the details. In any case, to make the best use of the program, you need to fiddle with it for yourself—futz with the various collections of icons and see what the different settings do on your machine.

So when I stop and recommend that you work through a dialog box on your own or read another source, that's not a cop-out. It's an introduction to a basic insight about using a computer:

Don't get mad, get even.

That is, if you don't like what the beast does, fiddle with it until you do—nine times in ten, you have a cure for the problem at your fingertips, but no one else can read your mind and tell you everything you need.

1 The Shortest Distance: A Concrete Example

Forget editing for a moment. Suppose you want to go from New York to San Francisco....

The most straightforward approach is to don a good pair of boots and start walking: go out the door and take the shortest combination of streets and roads that will get you there, cutting cross-country when you can. But it'd be a lot quicker to make plane reservations, call a cab, ride thirty miles in the wrong direction, dillyfrog around the airport for a couple of hours getting through security, and hike onto a commercial jet before you start moving in the direction you really want to go.

A plane shortens your travel time by getting above the obstacles and diversions of foot slogging, and by going very, very fast. A computer shortens your edit time by implementing your choices very, very quickly and tirelessly; it doesn't get bored going over the same stuff time and again, and it doesn't get irritated or make a mess if you change your mind.

So suppose you're working on a trade book in the social sciences whose authors have bolstered their observations with citations to a couple of hundred other published works. Your job—and it doesn't matter what tools you're using—is to confirm that every source in the reference section is cited somewhere in the text, every citation in the text leads to one source in the reference section, all the formatting is sound, and all the names and dates are consistent.

You can just edit the citations along with everything else—that is, pause whenever you get to one, tick it off on a copy of the reference list, and make whatever adjustments or queries it calls for. *Let's see, here's Williams on page 25 of the ref list ... here's Jensen—oops, Jenson—on page 10; gotta query that ... here's Morris on page 13 ... and here's Williams—is it the same Williams?—back on 25....* But it's not that bad; in fact, it probably takes no more than a minute per citation, and they often tend to cluster in parts of a document and leave other parts more or less without distractions.

But there are bunches and lots of them. Two hundred sources, cited an average of five times apiece in the manuscript; that's pushing a thousand minutes. More than fifteen hours. And that doesn't consider the time it will cost you to deal with the thirty-five or forty referenced sources that (probably) didn't get cited after all in the final draft, or the eighty-nine citations to sources that never got included or are so screwed up you can't be sure. Meanwhile, it's dangerous to skip checking a citation just because it looks familiar. Nine times out of ten, you may be right in figuring it's OK, but the tenth is going to have a misspelled name or erroneous date, and if you don't catch it, someone else probably will—and will wonder what sort of doofus did the edit.

(Yes, of course, I'm pulling numbers out of the air, here, and with an axe to grind besides. You can probably do it faster. But the bedrock truth remains: checking citations against references with everything on paper is a tedious and grueling chore.)

So what can the computer do for you here? If you treat the citations as a separate work unit, the computer can cut the overall time required to vet them all to a tiny fraction of the paper process. The main savings come from eliminating paper-shuffling; when you deal with all the citations to a source at once, you never have to go back to it. You also save time by automating much of the query process.

The steps involved are all dead easy, all computer-assisted, and many of them can be done in bulk rather than by fiddling with the citations one by one. For now, that's all you need to know about how they work. (You'll find explanations for all of them in later chapters. And these days, you can buy add-ins that automate parts of the process even further, but the do-it-yourself approach is useful as a capsule introduction to the philosophy of Word-whacking.)

Here's an overview of what you do:

1. *Make your plane reservations.* Jump from citation to citation, ignoring everything else.
    a. In each citation, fix any formatting errors you happen to notice. (It doesn't matter much if you miss something, but fixes now will be faster than fixes later.) If you see reliable patterns of error—say, the author uses "et al." and the client wants "and others"—close the documents you're working on and fix the errors for all the manuscript files at once.
    b. Copy each citation (or group of citations) and paste it into another file.
2. *Call a taxicab.* After you pull the citation copies for a whole chapter, make sure every citation is on a line of its own. Then label each with its chapter number at the end of the line.

3. *Go to the airport and make your way through security.* Once you have all the citations for the book copied, get them ready to check.
   a. Sort them by first author.
   b. Look over the list; if any author has so many items and coauthors that it's difficult to identify any of the works at a glance, do a further sort of that group by coauthor, by date, or both.
   c. Lay out the citation copies single-spaced and in two or three columns, to fit as many as possible on a page without sacrificing readability.
   d. Print them out on scratch paper.
4. *Get on the plane and fly.* Check the citations.
   a. Open the reference file.
   b. Put the printout in a comfortable spot near the screen, and vet each citation as you come to it on the list.
      (1) If it matches an entry in the reference file: Check it off on the printout.
      (2) If several citations match the same source: Make sure they really are identical, then draw one line through them to clear them as a group.
      (3) If a citation (or group of citations) has no matching reference: Open the indicated chapter or chapters and put a standard query at each citation.
      (4) If a reference has no citation: Have your computer check through the files to see if the author is mentioned anywhere. If you get any hits, open the indicated files and check to see if the source itself is mentioned in a nonstandard way that step 1 missed. If it's really not cited, put a standard query in the reference section, asking for citation or removal of the source.
      (5) If names or dates differ: Put more-or-less standard queries on both the citation and the reference entry.
      (6) If a citation has formatting errors: Open the indicated chapter file and fix them.

The details make these steps sound more complex than the ones required to take a plane instead of hiking cross-country, I know—but the detour really does make just as much difference to the amount of sweat involved in the journey. And this little book includes all the techniques you need to make it work. For pointers, just watch for the airplane notes like the one shown here, which will refer you to the appropriate numbered paragraphs in this chapter.

✈ paragraph #

2 Building a Working Environment

Well, you already have a working environment. The first trick is to find out what Word 2010 will do for you right now, with nothing added. Figure 1 gives you a quick look at your new friend.

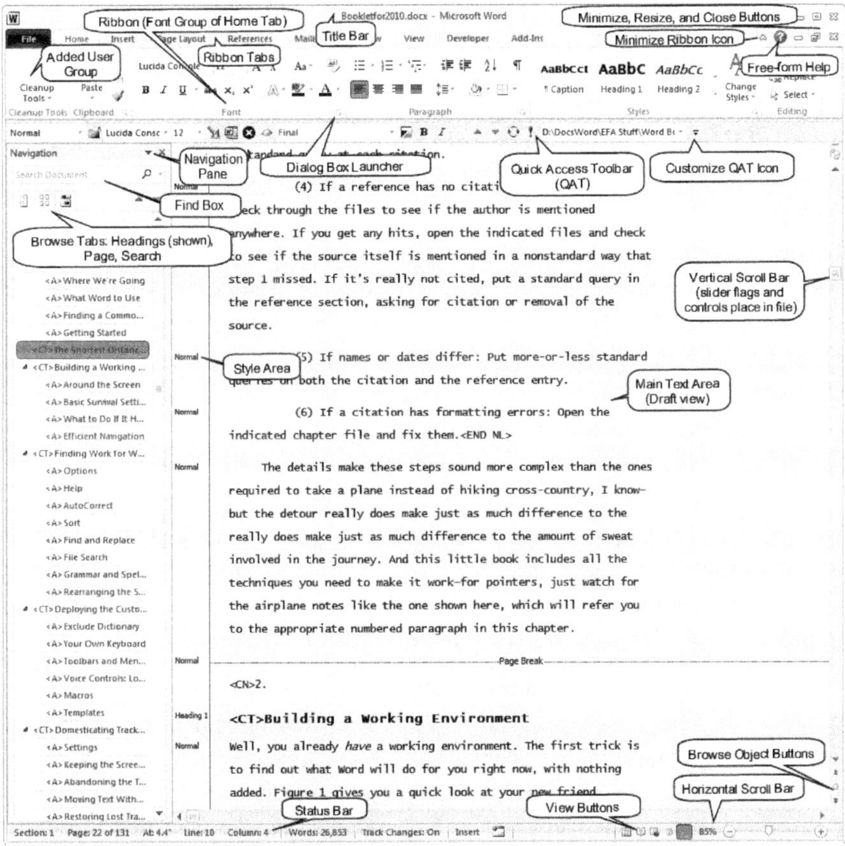

Figure 1. Main Elements of the Word 2010 Screen

Around the Screen

"My screen doesn't look like that!" you say. . . . No—but aside from having a draft of this book on it and a user group from one of my clients on the Home tab, it could. The callouts flag elements that you can choose to display. If you haven't changed any of Word's default settings, you won't see the panels on the left, and the Quick Access Toolbar (QAT) will be squeezed onto the title bar between the Word icon and the file name. The ribbon will lack a few of the tabs, too, but more on that later. The following sections give you detail on some of this stuff but don't describe everything labeled in the figure; I've flagged several additional items just to make sure I can talk about them later.

Status Bar

When you open Word for the first time, the Status bar at the bottom of the screen will be almost blank. But blank or full, it takes up the same amount of space, so you might as well make use of it. Figure 1 shows what I got by right-clicking anywhere on the Status bar and checking everything but "Formatted Page Number," which I generally leave turned off as being redundant with the "Page x of y" item when the document has only one series of page numbers.

Views

The view buttons let you change the appearance of the main text area. Figure 1 shows it in Draft view, which is where I spend most of my time, but you can also see whole pages complete with margins (Print Layout view), content as it would appear on the web (you got it, Web Layout view), two pages side by side like a paperback book (Full Screen Reading view), and an Outline view that lets you collapse and expand sections of the document and move stuff around without looking at it, which I've always found too scary to mess with. If you need to work in Print Layout view, you can conserve screen real estate by mousing over the space between the pages. When the pointer changes to a pair of little boxes with arrows, double-click to hide the blank space at the top and bottom of each page, along with any headers and footers. Mouse over and double-click again to get the margins (and headers and footers) back in sight.

Word 2010 stores your view settings with each file, so it will open in whatever state it was in when you saved it. If you care how new documents look when you create them (and you're not getting what you want), open Normal.dotm and adjust the view there, then save it. ("Using Templates" in chapter 5 explains how to get to Normal.dotm—what you knew as Normal.dot in earlier versions—and open it.)

Additionally, there's a Print Preview that shows you exactly what Word 2010 thinks your printer will do with the file, but it's not with the other view buttons—get it at Print on the File tab (still available as Alt+F, P), where it shows up beside the printer control boxes. Its biggest use is to check for bleeds and the lineup of two-page spreads, which you can see by changing the zoom percentage with the slider below the page image. It used to be possible to edit in Print Preview, but Word 2010 won't let you do that.

As I said, I prefer Draft view, switching to Print Layout view only to look for things that Draft hides: text boxes and other graphic elements. The old hot keys still work: Alt+V, N for Draft view—a survival from ancient days when it was called "Normal view"—and Alt+V, P for Print Layout view. With files fresh from a client, it's useful to switch to Print Layout view at least once early on, then drop the zoom factor (at the right side of the Status bar) down to 20 percent or so. You won't be able to read anything, but graphic elements will stand out like mold on cheese—especially if you follow the advice later in this chapter and change the white page background to a color that reduces the glare.

In addition, draft view allows you to wrap text when it reaches the edge of the screen, regardless of how the lines will actually break on the printed page. This means you can zoom in and out without ever having to scroll horizontally to see a full line of text. To set this up, go to File, Options (which you can still reach via Alt+T, O, just as if you were using the old Tools menu), Advanced, and check the box for "Show text wrapped within the document window" under "Show document content."

Style Area Pane

When you're in Draft view, this charming column tells you what style is assigned to each paragraph in the document. To open it, go to File, Options, Advanced, and mouse to the Display section, then type in a value next to "Style area pane width in Draft and Outline views." Keep the Style area closed if you don't care about styles, but it's worth half or three-quarters of an inch of screen real estate if the styles matter—especially if your client expects you to fix the styles as well as the text. In fact, if you have to play with styles, it's priceless; double-click on the name of a style there to open the Style dialog, where you can add, delete, and modify the little beasts.

> *Note:* Once the pane is open, you can change the width by hovering the pointer over the vertical line and using the double-headed arrow to drag it in or out. Dragging the margin all the way to the left closes the pane.

Navigation Pane

The Navigation pane, which contains three tabs, is a souped-up version of the old Document Map, plus some other useful goodies. Its formal home is in the Show group of the View tab, but you can open it by pressing the old hot-key combo for the Document Map: Alt+V, D. This combo will also switch to the Headings tab if one of the other tabs is on top at the moment. The Headings tab works about like the old Document Map, showing a hot-linked table of contents—based on the headings in the file but including elements from Outline view (including promoting and demoting headings from one level to another and selecting headings and their associated content). You can still expand and contract groups of headings and subheadings, using little black or white triangles instead of the plus and minus signs found in older versions of Word. Right-click anywhere in the list and choose "Show Heading Levels" from the context menu to specify the highest heading level (from 1 to 9) that you want to see on the list.

The Navigation pane also opens if you press Ctrl+F. Yes, that's the old hot key for the Find dialog, but now what it gets you is the Search tab, which will probably strike you as a pain in the tail the first few times you get there. But what it gives you can be glorious—a glimpse of all the places in the file where your search term appears, with a few words surrounding it, set up so you can jump to any of them and find the term highlighted in the text. And if you switch to the Headings tab with a search active (or start a search at that tab), the headings of sections containing the search term light up on the list, allowing you to pick the place likeliest to be what you want.

The center tab opens a set of page thumbnails that you can use to get around. They're too small to read but can come in handy if you're trying to find a graphic or some other layout element that stays visible when the page is shrunk to postage-stamp size. The key combo Alt+V, B opens this tab—and will also open the Navigation pane for you if it's closed at the moment.

Once the Navigation pane is open, you can switch from tab to tab by clicking the one you want.

Windows Taskbar

The Windows Taskbar isn't part of Word 2010 at all, but it's worth a bit of attention. It's a band along the bottom of the screen (of your primary monitor if you have more than one) that shows what programs you have running. You can control its appearance by right-clicking and then selecting Properties from the context menu; I set the "Taskbar buttons" drop-down list to "Never combine." With that setting, if you start the macro editor (discussed in chapter 5), you'll get a separate icon for that on the Taskbar, making it easy to click back and forth between Word and your macros.

You can have all your open Word files show up there separately; if you like that idea, go to File, Options, Advanced, Display and check "Show all windows in the Taskbar." This is the Word 2010 version of the Single Document Interface introduced in Word 2000, and I tend to leave the box unchecked unless I want to be able to compare two files side by side with one on each monitor. (Yes, I use two monitors—multiple monitors go from a luxury to a necessity in about the first forty-five seconds' experience.) The feature lost a bit in the course of being made optional: Word 2000 would stay open when you used the x in the top right corner to close the last file, but Word 2010 will shut down if you do that.

Ribbon Reassurance

For background, Figure 2 shows the top of the screen (including the ribbon) as it stands when Word 2010 has no customizations at all. chapter 4 goes into more detail on making the ribbon sit up and take notice, using a pic of my customized version as an example, but a couple of tips go a long way toward turning the ribbon into something you can live with.

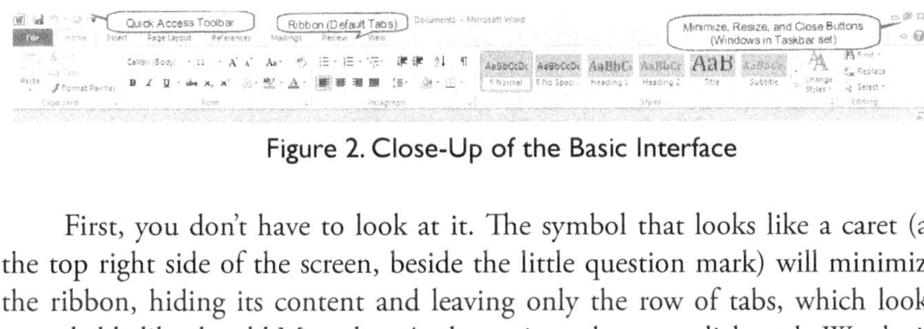

Figure 2. Close-Up of the Basic Interface

First, you don't have to look at it. The symbol that looks like a caret (at the top right side of the screen, beside the little question mark) will minimize the ribbon, hiding its content and leaving only the row of tabs, which looks remarkably like the old Menu bar. At that point, when you click a tab, Word will open that part of the ribbon so you can use its contents like a sort of super-menu, then close it and go back to the tab line when you return to your document. After you click the caret, it will invert itself into a tiny "V" shape: the Expand Ribbon icon, which opens the ribbon up again.

Second, there's more there than meets the eye. On many of the tabs, some of the groups have a peculiar little box shape at the lower right corner: the Dialog Box Launcher (flagged in Figure 1). Clicking it opens the dialog box that Word 2003 gave you for dealing with the topic addressed by the group. If you're sure you used to be able to do more with whatever-it-is than the ribbon doles out to you, click that little box, and the missing function will probably appear. (And if you have ScreenTips turned on—Alt+T, O; set ScreenTip style to "Show feature descriptions in ScreenTips"—Word 2010 will give you a thumbnail picture of the promised dialog box when you hover the pointer over the icon.)

The survival of these dialogs in the underlayers of Word 2010, like buried streets and chambers in an old, old city, is what allows after-market menu-restoration programs to do their thing. If the ribbon truly gives you hives, you can use something like Classic Menu for Office 2010 from http://www.addintools.com or ToolbarToggle from http://www.toolbartoggle.com to give you something like the old environment. But it really doesn't take all that long to get used to the new look. It's a nuisance to retool your brain if you already know where Word 2003 and its predecessors put things, but the new collections of tools are mostly quite logical. And with Word 2010, if something is really in the wrong place for the way your brain works, you can put it where you expect to find it by using the Customize Ribbon section of the Options dialog box on the File tab, reachable via Alt+T, O. (But I recommend leaving it in the old spot, in case someone who isn't you ever has to use your copy of Word….)

Quick Access to What You Really Want

The old Standard and Formatting toolbars are gone from Word 2010, which can feel like a dreadful loss. But they've been replaced by the free-form Quick Access Toolbar, on which you can hang anything you please. I keep the info boxes I use most there—style, font, font size, display, and a new one that lists the full path for the document location—plus assorted commands and macros that make my life easier. The style name box (which is hiding as Style on the All Commands list, one of the drop-down choices in the left column of the customize-QAT dialog) is especially useful, because it doesn't appear on any of the ribbon tabs; the Home tab has a complex Styles group that offers a whole package of styles but doesn't show what's on the page at the moment—and I've never had occasion to figure out what to do with it.

The little barred down-arrow at the end of the QAT opens the Customize Quick Access Toolbar menu, an old-fashioned drop-down list that presents several suggestions of things to add, a More Commands item that opens the full customize-QAT dialog box, and an item that lets you choose whether to show the QAT above the ribbon (sharing the title bar with the file name, as in Figure 2) or below it (taking up a whole new row on the screen, as in Figure 1). I prefer the latter as it provides more room for the QAT and brings the icons for the macros I keep there nearer the workspace. You can also get to the customize-QAT dialog at File, Options (Alt+T, O, Q).

The Amazing Dual-Purpose Alt Key

I keep referring to things that used to be on menus as "still available" by pressing Alt plus some other key, which may make it sound as though Word's designers had just kissed the Alt key good-bye and left it with the rest of the buried features. But that's not the case. Alt now has two completely separate ways to serve you.

If you think of a key combo you know well and just type it straight in, you get the old function of the key—whether it's one of the menu commands or one that you put in for yourself. But if you press Alt and then pause (as though to wonder what you should do next), the ribbon and QAT light up with letters and numbers in squares. Press (not click) any of those keys, and you get either the new function or a whole new array of squares offering more choices. This can repeat until you drill down to the specific item you want.

> *Note:* The File tab has completely eaten the old File menu, so Alt followed by F gets you to the same place regardless of how quickly you press the keys.

In the rest of this book, "Alt+[key]" refers to one of the old key combinations and means press both keys together. "Alt, [key]" refers to one of the new ones, meaning to press and release Alt, then press your selection from among the little squares that light up. But you won't see many of the new ones listed here; in general, I refer to things on the ribbon by using the whole series of tab and group names. If you want to use the new Alt codes, just press Alt and read the squares across the top of the ribbon. Press the one you want, then the one that lights up for the relevant group on that ribbon, and so on until you get the function you want. They're never going to be as efficient as the old key combos, though, because you can't just pound them in from memory; you have to wait for Word to give you the choices.

Actually, Alt has a third trick. Alt+drag allows you to move ruler tabs and text boxes without invoking the associated dialogs or snap-to-grid functions. If something won't stay where you want to keep it, try Alt-dragging it into place.

What to Do If It Hurts

Many people find that looking at the Word screen long enough to get anything done is outright painful, or at least so irritating that it's hard to see errors in the text. And the appearance of the text on the screen—especially the near-invisible punctuation marks—often cuts into editing accuracy. When this happens, the natural inclination is to retreat to paper and print the job out so you can work without suffering, but it's better to change the display instead.

The first thing to try is enlarging the text—in Word 2010, clicking the little plus sign at the right end of the Status bar, down at the bottom of your Word window. Many people find readability a simple matter of upping the magnification until the type is large enough to feel comfortable. (I don't, so I can't help suspecting that even those who think Zoom is an answer would be better off exploring other options before deciding on that approach.)

Taming the Display

If you haven't futzed with the settings, the default Word screen is the same as for most other programs controlled by your operating system: white background, black text. Within Word 2010, you can't really do anything about this without actually changing the colors in the file (in which case they'll print out); even the old "blue background, white text" option is gone, and the color schemes offered at File, Options, General just affect the ribbon and other sections surrounding the document. Instead, you have to go outside Word to fix the text and background colors you see.

Here's how it works in the two flavors of Windows that I've used recently. In Windows XP, the answer is to go to Control Panel, Display, Appearance, Advanced and reset the colors of all the screen elements to something you like to look at, then save the package as a "theme." In Windows 7, right-click on the desktop, click Personalize, and then click on Windows Classic for a display equivalent to the one described for Windows XP (see Figure 3). I'm not familiar with other operating systems, but they all should allow you some choice of display.

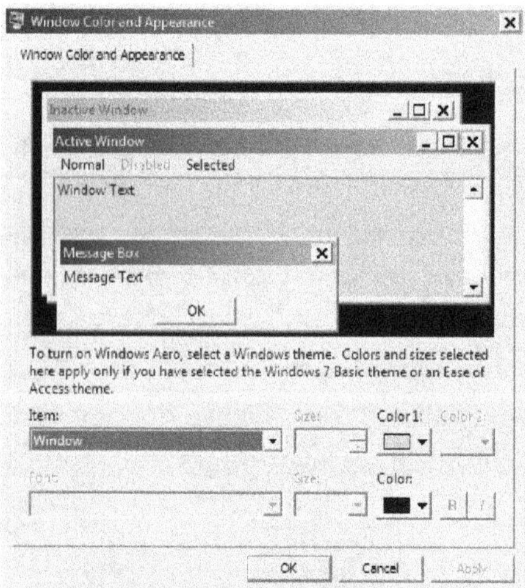

Figure 3. Window Color and Appearance Dialog

I like a slate blue working area with dark blue type, because high contrast makes my eyes itch. If your machine will run a Windows XP theme file and you'd like to see what I use, you can download a copy by entering http://www.powersedit.com/ftp/HScreens.zip on your web browser's address bar, making sure to get the uppercase and lowercase letters exactly as shown. Unzip the archive to get at the file itself. (It may instantly apply itself, but don't panic if that happens: it will also open the Windows Control Panel dialog that will let you unselect it.) For Windows 7, use http://www.powersedit.com/ftp/HScreens7.zip instead. Windows XP will find the theme file no matter where you put it on your hard drive, but under Windows 7 it has to be in Users/[your username]/AppData/

Local/Microsoft/Windows/Themes. If this path doesn't seem to exist on your computer, go to the Windows Control Panel and click Folder Options, View, and set the "Show hidden files and folders" radio button to on; and be sure to uncheck "Hide extensions for known file types." (These features are under Appearance and Personalizations if you're using the Category view of the Control Panel.)

> *Note:* The process of unzipping archives will vary depending on your computer setup. Right-click the file name in Windows Explorer, and click your unzip utility or "Extract All," which will appear if you don't have another utility integrated with Windows. If you don't see "Extract All" you can still get to the same function by highlighting "Open with >" and choosing "Compressed (zipped) folders" in Windows XP or "Windows Explorer" in Windows 7 from the next menu that opens. If you don't have a utility and want to be able to make zip archives of your own, see "Compression Managers" in chapter 8, under "Other Support Programs."

My choice isn't the one true best way for everybody, of course; about half the people who see it like it, and many of the rest want to run screaming. But if you find your eyes getting tired while you work, the hard black-and-white screen may be the culprit—even if it hasn't occurred to you that it might be a problem. If that's the case, the only way you'll find out is to play with the screen for yourself.

Getting Text You Can Read

Font choice is almost as individual as display environment. The original Windows default font, Times New Roman, is dense and reasonably handsome, so most people stay with it, but I find it a disaster for editing. Part of its problem is built-in authority (it looks so much like a printed book, even the errors seem to make sense), and the rest is that it's so dense—and the punctuation marks are so small in comparison to the letters—that it's just plain hard to see details. Calibri, the new default, is much prettier but still somewhat cramped. Courier (now Courier New) is the traditional typewriter-style font, and many publishers still use it for manuscript files. My own favorite is Lucida Console, which is denser than Courier New but looks more open, and I do all my work in 12-point Lucida Console zoomed down to 85 percent, switching back to the client's preference before returning a job. (See "Template Tips and Tricks" in chapter 5 for more on how to do this without manually changing the font.) In this book, the screen shots that show bits of a file give you a glimpse of Lucida Console, but don't judge it by that—it's a pure screen font and not particularly agreeable on paper.

Note: If your work involves non-Roman alphabets or mathematical symbols, check your chosen font for compatibility. Make sure what you see makes sense, and if it doesn't—or you wouldn't know sense from nonsense—look at an unmodified copy of the original file to see if it matches.

Once again, there's no one best way—but there'll be something you like better than the other choices open to you, and it probably won't be anything a client sends you. With paper, you have to take what you get, but on the screen you can suit yourself.

Visual Aids

Still another choice involves what you see on the screen—just the letters and punctuation marks, or all of that plus what Word refers to as "hidden text": codes that indicate where the spaces and tabs and some other things are sitting. You can turn the display of hidden text on and off by clicking the pilcrow (¶) on the Home tab of the ribbon, or by pressing Ctrl+Shift+8. File, Options, Display includes check boxes that let you specify individual codes to show all the time.

I tend to leave hidden text turned off all the time, except when I need to see what's happening at that level.

Efficient Navigation

For real editing speed, the keyboard beats the mouse for almost everything. (After all, which is faster: moving your hand off the keyboard or not moving your hand off the keyboard?) So it's a good idea to learn and use the keyboard shortcuts (also called "hot keys") for the things you do most often, and the arrow and movement keys to get around the file. Here are some of the basics:

Alt, brief pause, anything that lights up on the QAT or ribbon: Press the number or letter indicated to do what you want. (Sometimes a two-character code will light up; this means to press those two in sequence.)

[Arrow Key] alone: Move one character or line in the direction of the arrow per key press.

Ctrl+[Arrow Key]: Move one word or paragraph in the direction of the arrow per key press. (If you're in the middle of a paragraph, the up-arrow will move to the beginning of that paragraph.)

Shift+[Arrow Key]: Select one character or line in the direction of the arrow per key press.

Shift+Ctrl+[Arrow Key]: Select one word or paragraph in the direction of the arrow per key press. (If you're in the middle of a paragraph, the up- and down-arrows will select the remainder of that paragraph.)

Home or *End alone*: Move to the beginning or end of the line, respectively.

Shift+Home or *Shift+End*: Select to the beginning or end of the line, respectively.

Ctrl+Home or *Ctrl+End*: Move to the beginning or end of the file, respectively.

Shift+Ctrl+Home or *Shift+Ctrl+End*: Select to the beginning or end of the file, respectively.

Ctrl+[click]: Select the sentence where the cursor is located, plus the following space, if any.

Shift+F5: Go back to the last action; on open, go to the place where the cursor was located when the file was saved. If you press the combination repeatedly while you're working, it will cycle through the last four places it registered (with your current location as number 4 if you don't get too clever along the way), which will usually turn out to be changes to the text or the results of Find operations. Ctrl+Alt+Z will do the same thing; so will Ctrl+PageUp and Ctrl+PageDown as long as the browse object is set to Browse by Edits. (Click the little open circle below the vertical scroll bar to select the browse object; hover over the double arrows above or below the circle to see the current setting.)

> *Note:* Shift+F5 is great when it works, but it often doesn't—especially when you want to go somewhere, fix a couple of things, and return. Chances are, the checkpoints will all concentrate in the new location, and you'll lose the pointer back to where you were working.
>
> I wound up recording two macros: SetPlace, which puts a bookmark named Place at the current location of the cursor, and GoPlace, which moves the cursor to the Place bookmark. On Alt+F5 and Ctrl+F5, respectively, they provide a pretty good go-back function—immune to the troubles that beset Shift+F5, but of course subject to foresight errors; you have to set Place before you need it. (See chapter 5 for the basics on macros.)

3 Finding Work for Word's Idle Hands

Like all its predecessors, Word 2010 has a built-in desire to *do things* for its users. When you don't want what it thinks you should want, it's endlessly annoying—grating on your nerves like a hyper-controlling parent telling you what to wear and what to say. But you can almost always make it stop and remember to stay stopped, and once you get past its "Word Knows Best" approach, what remains is flexible and genuinely helpful.

Options

How to make it get its nose out of your business? The details would fill a book like this one, but the first step boils down to getting acquainted with all the options lists—the ones on the File tab (which I still access with Alt+T, O), the AutoCorrect options (which open happily with Alt+T, A, though you can also get them at File, Options, Proofing), and the Track Changes options (on the down-arrow beside Track Changes on the Review tab; if they have a hot key, I haven't found it—and I don't change them often enough to make it worth building one). Open a garbage file (any file you don't care about), then start working through the choices. (You'll see a number of specific suggestions about settings throughout this book, but there's no one best way for everyone. If there were, Word would be a lot simpler.)

One quick rule of thumb: When Word calls something "smart," it means "I'm smart and you're not." Except for smart—that is, curly—quotes, I leave all the smartness turned off. I also try to suppress all the arrays of choices Word 2010 loves to offer if it suspects it knows what you're doing. I've never managed to nail all of them all the time, but unchecking "Show Mini Toolbar on selection" at File, Options, General is a good start, as is unchecking "Show Paste Options button when content is pasted" in the "Cut, copy, and paste" section of File, Options, Advanced.

If you don't know what something does, try turning it off and seeing whether Word's behavior changes; you can always turn it back on again if you don't like the results or if you see no apparent change. If you don't see any change and decide to leave something turned off, make a note of what you changed—that way, you have a good start for troubleshooting if something unfortunate shows up later.

Buried at the end of the File, Options, Advanced list, under the Compatibility options, is a button labeled "Layout Options." That opens a list of finicky points—a few dozen of them—that you can check off to control the appearance of Word documents in subtle ways. They're all unchecked by default, and I generally leave them that way, but you might find it worth experimenting there if you're trying to push Word 2010 beyond word processing and into desktop publishing. For instance, the item that reads "Do full justification the way WordPerfect 6.x for Windows does" produces a paragraph with somewhat better spacing than the native Word algorithm can make—but an editor rarely has to worry about justified text, anyway. I leave that sort of thing to the page-makeup folks.

Keepers: At File, Options, General, set ScreenTip style to "Show feature descriptions in ScreenTips" (which tells Word to tell you what something is when you hover the pointer over it); at File, Options, Display, turn on "Show document tooltips on hover" (which turns on useful commentary about who did what and when); and at File, Options, Advanced, Editing options, turn on "Show AutoComplete suggestions" (which lets Word offer to fill in things like the days of the week for you).

Help

You can consult the Help system to find out about mystery options. The Help system in Word 2010, accessed via F1 or the free-form question mark in the upper right corner of the screen, can be genuinely helpful—though it feels a little shakier to me than the one in Word 2003 (and some online posters assert that it's awful). It's sometimes a challenge to figure out what Word calls whatever it is you want to ask about, but it's worth a try. Before you ask someone else (say, on a discussion list) for aid, put a brief version of the query into the search box at the top of the Help dialog—you may get a useful answer.

Alternatively, you could turn to a search engine. Online resources have achieved a scope and depth sufficient to answer almost any question you can think of—and usually provide a how-to video, too.

AutoCorrect

The AutoCorrect Options dialog box (in File, Options, Proofing, but more quickly available at Alt+T, A) still has five powerful tabs—but two are different from earlier versions. Old enemies are the two AutoFormat tabs, where Word hides some of its most annoying compulsive helpfulness; I keep almost everything there turned off, except for curly quotes, built-in heading styles, and tables. The Actions tab (which replaces the Smart Tags introduced in Word 2002) seems to be less invasive than its predecessor; I haven't had any trouble from it, so my copy has the defaults turned on.

The AutoCorrect tab tells Word to replace what you type with something else specified in its list. Once you prune the defaults to get rid of things that cause you trouble—like changing "(c)" to the copyright symbol, ©, which is a pain when you're trying to make an in-line list—it is vastly useful, and you don't have to give up the defaults entirely. I use "(c))" for the copyright symbol, for instance. You can assign text of your own to AutoCorrect by selecting the text, then going to the AutoCorrect Options dialog box, clicking the AutoCorrect tab, and typing in the trigger characters you plan to use for this text. The new Math AutoCorrect tab provides a convenient way to enter Greek letters and mathematical symbols into your text; if you need such things often, memorize the ones you use.

AutoCorrect is best for short phrases that need no formatting. (It will do formatted text, but I found that part of the feature unreliable in earlier versions and therefore have ignored it in Word 2010.) The most efficient way to use it is to check "Replace text as you type" on the tab, but if you do that, be careful to avoid using regular words as triggers. For example, if I type "ip," my copy of Word instantly changes it to "Is the preceding sentence OK?" (the query opener I use most often). You wouldn't want to use "is" for that purpose.... It doesn't tie you up completely, though; if you trigger an AutoCorrect item you don't want, press Ctrl+Z (Undo the last action) immediately, and it will go back to what you typed.

Other handy AutoCorrect items to get you started:

- thp = the preceding sentence
- th2 = the two preceding sentences
- thpa = this paragraph
- thpb = the preceding paragraph
- thpn = the next paragraph

It's useful to keep a list of your AutoCorrect collection, so that you can restore it smoothly if the active copy gets corrupted. Word 2010 has no built-in command to print the list for you, but Allen Wyatt's Word Tips came up with a macro that does the job. At any rate, it drops the list into the current Word document, which you can then save or print. It was designed for pre-2007 editions of Word, but it still works in 2010. You can pick it up at http://word.tips.net/Pages/T000340_Printing_a_List_of_AutoCorrect_Entries.html (http://tinyurl.com/PrintAutoCorrect). Alternatively (or as well), you can make a copy of the AutoCorrect file and keep it safe—which will also let you move your list to another computer. Look in C:\Users\[your username]\AppData\Roaming\Microsoft\Office (Windows 7) or C:\Documents and Settings\[your username]\Local Settings\Application Data\Microsoft\Office (Windows XP) for a file named MSO####.acl—where #### is a number that designates your language preference. (U.S. English is MSO1033.acl.) For more info, see http://www.word-2010.com/move-autocorrect-entries-in-word-to-a-new-computer (http://tinyurl.com/MoveAutoCorr).

You won't find an AutoText tab on the AutoCorrect dialog anymore, but the feature isn't gone. It's now in Quick Parts on the Insert tab of the ribbon, and the choices involved are complex enough to be best discussed in the next chapter, after I've introduced templates.

Sort

Things happen. The author stuck things into the bibliography without reading their neighbors carefully enough. The style sheet wants you to put all the special vocabulary in alphabetical order. The elements of a table need resequencing. When you need to put things in a certain order, Word is there to help.

The sorting tool Word gives you will sort items on a list or longer paragraphs either by the first word or by subsequent words (or by delimited fields) for a whole file or a block of text you select, and it will sort on up to three different parts of an item at a time. Word 2010 puts the Sort Text dialog on the Home tab of the ribbon, using a moderately clear icon (A over Z with an arrow) in the Paragraph group. It will also sort table columns for you, and you can still get it with Alt+A, S—the key combo for its old location on the Table menu. The options differ somewhat depending on what kind of material you're working with, so the best thing to do is open a garbage file and play with it.

The example in chapter 1 uses Sort to get the citation copies into the same order as the reference section. The second-level sort is sometimes faster if you just horse the lines around with Cut and Paste (Ctrl+X and Ctrl+V), but Sort can come in handy again here as well.

→ 3.a-b

Find and Replace

To get at this most helpful facility, press Ctrl+H to open the Replace tab of the Find and Replace dialog box, and then click the More button or press Alt+M to see the whole thing. (The stripped-down default version of this dialog box is another of Microsoft's stupider ideas, and there's no built-in option to keep it open from one session to the next. However, uber-Word-whacker David Chinell teamed up with Word MVP Jay Freedman to produce a brilliant pair of macros that does the job—untouched by human hand—every time. See "Getting More without Asking" in chapter 9.)

Explore the Format and Special buttons, which will give you a good idea of the kinds of things you can do beyond typing before-and-after text on the "Find what" and "Replace with" lines. Experiment with the keyboard shortcuts for formatting—most of them work as three-way toggles on both lines. Ctrl+Shift+[plus sign], for example, toggles from "Superscript" to "Not Superscript/Subscript" to no reference to superscripting, and Ctrl+B and Ctrl+I do the same for boldface and italics. If you look for one type of formatting and change it to another without specifying any text, Word will just change the formatting, but the "Replace with" line has to specify that you don't want the old formatting. Changing boldface to italics gets you bold italics unless you use the "Not Bold" toggle on the "Replace with" line.

Even though the old Find shortcut, Ctrl+F, now goes to the Navigation pane Search tab, the dialog it used to open is still there. You can get to that section of the Find and Replace dialog box after pressing Ctrl+H by clicking the Find tab, or pressing Alt+D. Its main use these days is to select a group of items scattered through the file—the first-level headings, for example—so you can copy and paste them all as a group. It will also allow you to apply formatting to your found items all at once, if you're sure enough of your search criteria to change them sight unseen.

> *Note:* Word 2010 makes the grab-a-group trick harder than it used to be, as the Find dialog no longer has a Find All button. The Reading Highlight button that replaced it does nothing but highlight the found items; you can't copy what it highlights. Instead, you need to click the down-arrow on the Find In button and choose "Main Document"; that will make Word select a group you can copy. (Just press Esc to dismiss the dialog box after you run the find operation, then press Ctrl+C without clicking in the document to copy what Word found.)

The Replace tab is useful for almost everything else you might want to do, whether or not you have actual replacement in mind. For instance, it will find the first instance of your search term and *stop without changing it* whether you click Find Next or Replace; you need to click Replace again after something has been found to get it to change. And spend some time looking at the underlined letters on the dialog box; they all work like the menu items in Word 2003: press Alt plus the underlined letter to get the effect promised, which is apt to be quicker than mousing to the item in question. (The Find tab offers a similar set of shortcuts, of course, but you're not there when you open the dialog.)

My only real beef with the dialog has to do with its Alt+T shortcut, which has two different uses: to search for a suffix, and to remove all formatting from a search. If you haven't been using the dialog to look for formatting (italics, highlighting, whatever), it provides a simple on/off toggle to search for words with the suffix you specify on the "Find what" line. However, if you search for formatting and then decide to clear it from the search string, you have to press Alt+T *three times*: first it turns on the "Match suffix" box, then it turns off the look-for-formatting provision, then it turns off the "Match suffix" box—and *then* you can go on with your search operation.

Word 2010 will (usually) find anything you can describe in a file, and replace it with anything you say you want, either one instance at a time or for a whole file, and you can even buy an add-in that will expand its efforts to a whole directory (see "Editorium" in chapter 8). For example, you can use it for simple nuisances like extra spaces. Hide tracked changes (so Word doesn't keep finding spaces it already deleted) by choosing the "Final" option in the Display for Review drop-down box in the Tracking group of the Review tab, then:

- *Find what*: [space][space] (meaning that you should type two spaces, not the words in the brackets or the brackets themselves)
- *Replace with*: [space]
- *Click*: Replace All (or press Alt+A) to do a global change, that is, to change every instance of two spaces to a single space without pausing for you to look at it.

You may have to do this more than once, to eliminate the remains of triple spaces and other excesses. The white space special character (^w, where the ^ is the character you can type with Shift+6 on most keyboards) is a bigger hammer—use it to get rid of all multiple spaces in one pass if you don't mind losing all your tabs at the same time.

At the other end of the scale, you can use Replace to install text that contains internal formatting—H_2O, for example, or *im*possible (which is what I used to think this trick was)—in one pass. Simply format one instance of the text the way you want to see it, then select it and press Ctrl+C to copy it to the Clipboard. Then set up the dialog like this:

- *Find what*: [the text you plan to replace with your formatting, either pasted from the Clipboard (the formatting won't matter here) or another string—"water," for example]
- *Replace with*: ^c (the special character for the full contents of the Clipboard—say, H_2O—including the formatting, which won't normally show up in the dialog box)
- *Click*: Replace (or press Alt+R) to find and change one instance at a time, or Replace All (or press Alt+A) to do a global change.

This trick works only in one direction; you can't use it to find specifically formatted text while ignoring strings of the same characters without formatting. Word 2010 still refuses to take the ^c special character on the "Find what" line.

You can also use Find and Replace for weirder and more complex things, feeding it *wildcards* (codes that look for classes of things or patterns rather than specific characters) and telling it to find all instances that fit the specified pattern, and then change something next to them while preserving the pattern itself. For example, if you have a reference section where all the authors' initials are run together—A.B. Smith, C.D. Jones, and so on—and your client wants them spaced out, wildcard replace will let you go in and separate all the initials without putting a bunch of spaces where you don't want them. Here's how that would look:

- *Find what*: ([A-Z]).([A-Z])
- *Replace with*: \1.[space]\2 (again, using an actual space, not the word or the square brackets)
- *Check*: "Use wildcards" under Search Options
- *Click*: Replace (or press Alt+R) for each instance found

For more, see Table 1: Principal Wildcard Characters and What They Do.

By the by, the tip in Table 1 about using ^013 to search for a hard return can come in handy even when you're not using wildcards. Every once in a while, a file turns out to have hard returns that the regular Find refuses to see, even though they look like any other pilcrow if you turn on hidden characters. When that

Table 1: Principal Wildcard Characters and What They Do

Location in the Replace Dialog	Character	Action	Example
"Find what" box	?	Look for any single character	m?n (finds "man" and "men" but not "mean")
"Find what" box	*	Look for any string	m*n (finds "man," "men," and "mean," as well as anything else beginning and ending with those letters, whether or not they occur at the beginnings or ends of words)
"Find what" box	[ ]	Designate a wildcard string	[A-Z] (finds any uppercase character)
"Find what" box	( )	Flag a wildcard string for reference in the "Replace with" box	([A-Z])
"Find what" box	{ }	Set a number of occurrences to look for, where n and m are digits	{n} (finds exactly n of the preceding character or expression) {n,} (finds at least n) {n,m} (finds from n to m)
"Find what" box	^013	Look for a hard return (^p doesn't work with wildcards)	See next example
"Find what" box	!	Limit the Find operation to strings that do not contain the following characters	([!.])^013 (finds a hard return not preceded by a period)
"Find what" box	\	Look for the following character as a character, even if it's usually one of the specials	([!.:\)])^013 (finds a hard return not preceded by a period, a colon, or a right parenthesis)
"Find what" box	A-Z	Specify the range of uppercase letters	
"Find what" box	a-z	Specify the range of lowercase letters	
"Replace with" box	\n	Refer to the nth element in parentheses in the "Find what" box	In the "A.B. Smith" example, \2.[space]\1 would reverse the initials to "B. A."

happens, a regular (non-wildcard) global replace of ^013 with ^p will probably open Word's eyes for you.

I return to wildcards at the end of the "Removing Tracking from an Edited File" section of chapter 6, as they bear on the technique under discussion there. And for a much better description of Word's wildcards than I have space for here, check out the archives of Jack Lyon's *Editorium Update* newsletter at http://www.editorium.com/archive/htm.

The key articles are in March, April, and May 2001—which may seem old, but the concepts have not changed since then—and a search on "wildcards" will reveal additional bits of interesting information.

> *Warning:* Wildcards and Track Changes do not play well together, and it's usually necessary to turn off the latter to use the former successfully. That makes most global wildcard replace actions a whole lot scarier than I want to deal with; without the tracking, it's way too easy to miss the need to change something back if the operation "fixed" it improperly. So it's best to click the Replace button for each change you know you want unless things are very, very clear.

→ 1.

The example in chapter 1 uses Find in a couple of different ways. When it talks about jumping from one citation to the next, what's actually happening is a search for open parentheses. Put a ")" on the "Find what" line and click the Find Next button, then press the Esc key to close the dialog box. Look for subsequent instances by pressing Ctrl+PageDown. This ploy takes advantage of the convention whereby almost every citation has a set of parentheses somewhere in it—either around the whole thing or just around the date. If the parens are being used for something other than a citation, just press Ctrl+PageDown again (or Ctrl+PageUp to go back if you run past a spot where you should have stopped).

→ 4.b(3-6)

Later, when the example talks about looking through files to find specific citations, you would get that effect by pasting the author's name (or the whole citation) into the "Find what" line, then using that to search the indicated chapters for the citation in question.

→ 2.

The example also uses the Replace facility, first to separate groups of citations by replacing the semicolons and spaces that appear in citation clusters—(Smith, 1994; Jones, 2001; Abelskiver, 1984)—with hard returns:

- *Find what*: [semicolon][space]

- *Replace with*: ^p (the special character used in this tool to designate a paragraph break)

Then add the chapter numbers to the citations:

- *Find what*: ^p
- *Replace with*: [space][chapter #]^p (again, leaving out the square brackets, and using the actual number of the chapter rather than the "chapter #" placeholder)

One more trick: If your author repeatedly confuses common words—"form" and "from," for example, or "than" and "then" (or "that")—use Find and Replace to flag the members of a pair with different colors. That will boost your chances of noticing when they're wrong, which is amazingly difficult while you're editing and dead easy for anyone just reading the material.

- *Find what*: [one of the problem words]
- *Check*: "Find whole words only"
- *Replace with*: [no text, Highlight] (that is, click More, Format, Highlight)
- *Click*: Replace all

Then go up to the Font group of the Home tab on the ribbon, click the down-arrow on the Highlight icon (the one with "ab" and a crayon, with a colored bar under it), pick another color, and repeat this Find and Replace operation for the other member of the pair. At the end of the job, select the whole file and set the highlighting to None.

Find and Replace is great stuff—but bear in mind that the original genie in a bottle has nothing on Word for literal-minded obedience, so you have to be very, very careful with it. The basic survival rule:

Never run a global change on a file you won't read again.

You don't want to find out in page proofs that fixing the author's obsessive use of "may" instead of the correct "can" has left things canbe happening on Can 15....

And one sad drawback:

You can't completely trust Find.

Things sometimes happen in Word's innards to prevent it from finding things you can see on the screen, large as life and twice as ugly. Tracked changes can contribute to the problem but aren't the whole of it. Problems are much rarer with Word 2010 than they were when I started editing in Word 95, but it feels like a good idea to warn you that it ain't perfect. If you ask it to find two consecutive spaces and it reports there aren't any, even though you can see some, of course you're right and it's wrong. Word Happens. Don't worry about it—it really is rare. Think of it as one more reason the computer will stay a tool instead of trying to take over for you.

File Open

The File, Open dialog—on the File tab, but easier to reach at Ctrl+F12 or Ctrl+O—will reward some study. It does more for you than simply open files. Figure 4 shows the dialog as it appears in Windows XP and Windows 7.

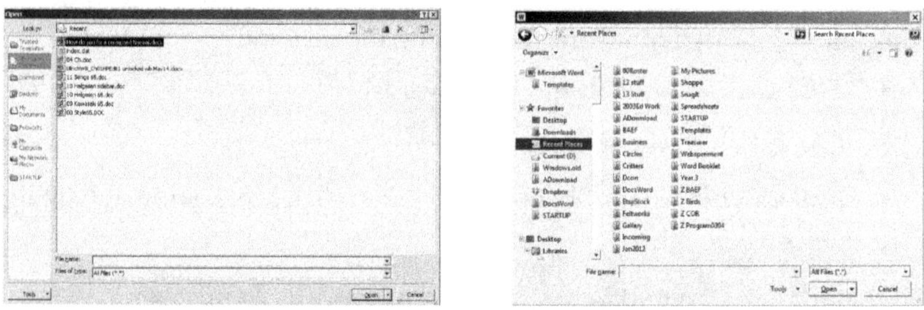

Figure 4. File Open:
Windows XP and Windows 7

First of all, it can make your life easier by starting out with the files you're most likely to want. Set the default look-in directory by going to File, Options, Advanced, General (which is toward the end of the list) and clicking the File Locations button, then setting Documents to wherever you've put your files by clicking the Modify button. (If you're using the default, you're home and dry, but if you've put your data and your operating system on different physical or logical drives, you'll need to change it here.) There's another trick to getting the Windows 7 search box on this screen to work the way you want it to, but that's complex enough to deal with in the next section.

The left pane on the File, Open dialog box looks quite different depending on your operating system. In Windows 7, it starts with the templates directory, then essentially replicates the left pane in Windows Explorer: your Favorites, followed by a section called Desktop. In Windows XP, it looks more like what Word 2003 gave you, listing some default items plus whatever you add, in the order you arrange it, but it will still begin with the Templates directory.

The rest of the dialog box differs a lot between operating systems, though the same functions are on offer. Here are the ones I find most useful:

Folder View. You can change the presentation of information about files by clicking a down-arrow in the upper right corner. In Windows 7, it's the second symbol to the left of the question mark; in Windows XP it's at the far right. I like to keep it on "List" to get the most file names onto the screen. However, the "Preview" option (included on the XP drop-down menu; accessed by the icon between the down-arrow and the question mark in Windows 7) lets you look inside a closed file, which can come in handy when you're checking chapter titles or other details of the openers.

Recover Text. The down-arrow beside "Files of type" in Windows XP and on the unnamed box that defaults to "All files (*.*)" in Windows 7 drops down a fairly predictable list of file types, plus—buried in the middle—"Recover Text from Any File," which can bring up the semantic content plus some historical information at the cost of losing all the formatting. To use it, highlight a .doc file name in the main list, then click the relevant down-arrow to get to your choice. (It turns out that "any file" is a bit of a misnomer, however—with a .docx file, it gets nothing but gibberish.)

Open and Repair. The down-arrow beside the Open button (in either operating system) includes several rarely useful choices, plus one labeled "Open and Repair," which can sometimes remove enough corruption to get you into a file that wants to crash your system. To use it, highlight a file name in the main list, then click the relevant down-arrow to get to your choice.

File Search

"Didn't this author say something like this before, only different?"

Spatial memory—the ability to know that something that bears on the edit at point B was first mentioned at point A … two inches back up the stack of paper and about a third of the way down the page—is among the most refined and valuable skills of on-paper editing. Going straight to what you want is both admirable and pleasurable, and many a reluctantly electronic editor has bemoaned the impossibility of exercising this skill on screen, where it feels like you're peering through a toilet-paper roll at a tiny fragment of the manuscript.

With electronic editing, the spatial part of spatial memory is gone; you really can't lay an eyeball on the whole manuscript. But the memory part still matters. When something makes you twitch, you can have your computer hunt through the manuscript files and tell you where the keywords you'd look for by eye on paper are to be found. (Of course, if the whole manuscript is contained in one file, you can use the ordinary Find techniques already discussed.)

Word itself no longer has a File Search command like the one built into Word 2003 and earlier versions, so exactly how you go about using this facility depends on your operating system. The two I know anything about are Windows XP and Windows 7, but I'd be surprised if any operating system that could run Word 2010 didn't have something equivalent.

In Windows XP, use Search in Windows Explorer. (This is a different beast from Internet Explorer; get it at Start, All Programs, Accessories, Windows Explorer—and then put shortcuts wherever you're likely to look for it: Start, the desktop, the Quick Launch area. Alternatively, if your keyboard has a Windows key—the one with the little Windows logo on it—pressing Windows+E will open the Explorer right up.) Highlight the directory containing the files you want to look through, click the Search button on the toolbar, click "All files and folders," then paste the term you want to trace on the "Word or phrase in the file" line, and turn it loose. (You'd think it'd be faster to specify .docx files, since that's what you're looking for, but that option forces you into a second dialog to get to the search-for-text bit.)

In Windows 7, file search is set up to be very easy. The File, Open dialog in Word 2010 has a box in the upper right corner that offers to search your current directory for you, but it has a couple of peculiar gotchas. To make it search for a phrase without requiring AND and OR and the rest of the Boolean operators, go to Folder Options on the Windows Control Panel, and select "Use natural language search" in the Search tab. If you're using the Category view of the Control Panel, you'll find Folder Options under Appearance and Personalization. And if you've put your document files anywhere but the default C: drive location, adjust the look-in libraries by clicking "location" (or "locations") on the "Libraries" section of the File, Open dialog, which you can get to via the Desktop section of the left pane of the File, Open dialog. (The same Search box appears on the Windows Explorer window, replacing the toolbar Search button in Windows XP—but it's simpler to use the one in Word. But if you do want Windows Explorer, it's still available by pressing Windows+E.)

Regardless of your operating system, of course, you can also open each file and use Find to search for the word or phrase; it's slower, but it works and may be easier to understand. And it's not all that much slower, if you use the Search Document line and Search tab on the Navigation pane, which will give you a few words around

→ 4.b(4)

each appearance of the word or phrase you're looking for—an effect very like eyeballing your way through a paper manuscript.

The example in chapter 1 uses the file search facility to look for authors of sources that appear to be uncited in the text.

Language Settings

Word 2010 brings the choice of language indoors, so to speak, so you can get (and fix) all the settings you need without going outside the program the way you had to with Word 2003. It has abandoned the assumption that you want your system rearranged the instant you peek at a non-Roman font. The main language settings are in the Options dialog of the File tab (Alt+T, O, L), as well as under Language on the Review ribbon (where you'll find a screen to set the language of selected text). As always, you can use the Find and Replace dialog to locate and fix bits of text that have come in tagged with other languages (so Word thinks they're not supposed to follow the rules for English)—something particularly common in reference lists, where authors often copy suggested wording to the Clipboard and allow settings from the source document to come along.

Grammar and Spelling Checkers

As it comes out of the box, Word 2010 (hyperhelpful as ever) wants to keep an eye on your grammar and your spelling for you and put squiggly lines of various colors under anything it thinks may be wrong. However, it gives you the option of running the checkers on demand. I've turned all the real-time checking off—I want to think about spelling when I want to think about it, not when Word wants me to think about it—and I've turned off the grammar checker entirely. (To control these settings, go to File, Options, Proofing—still available at Alt+T, O, from the vanished Tools, Options dialog.)

Grammar Check Bad

Word can't *read*. It can only recognize some patterns of words, and the grammar checker is wrong more often than it's correct, both for what it identifies as an error and for what it proposes as a replacement. It's distinctly unsafe to consult the grammar checker unless your grasp of grammar is so solid that you really don't need it—and at that point, why bother? If you have particular things you want to look for—extra-long sentences, for instance—you can customize the grammar checker settings to look for those and ignore everything else, but I haven't found even that worthwhile since I parted from the one client I knew would look at the statistics and judge the edit by them.

The preceding paragraph describes my experience through Word 2003, so I turned on the grammar checker in Word 2010 and had it review this manuscript up to this point. Nothing has changed. Word flagged no real errors. Instead, it picked up on a lot of sentence fragments that I'd used for dramatic effect, plus several alleged fragments that weren't. It was also outright wrong on a dozen phrases, suggesting I exchange good grammar for bad. The funniest of these had to do with my AutoCorrect-powered query opener "ip": Word recommended replacing "Is the preceding sentence OK?" with "Be the preceding sentence OK?" At the Renaissance Faire, maybe….

Spelling Check Good

The spelling checker, by contrast, is useful … though still not entirely safe. Mostly what it tells you is that a word is not in its dictionary, and then it proposes alternatives with similar spelling. That is, if the file says *tu*, Word will suggest "too" and "to" and "tub" and "tug" and a few others—but it can't tell which would be right, or even alert you when *tu* is correct for the Latin expression the author was quoting. (It does have some language settings other than English, but you'll rarely see them used in any way you'll find helpful unless you work in multilingual documents.)

Word 2010 can do a bit more than earlier versions. If you check the "Use contextual spelling" box on the File, Options, Proofing dialog, the spelling checker will report potential problems if a word doesn't seem to match the part of speech required at that point in the text, rather than simply accepting any word in its dictionary. This can occasionally save your bacon, but—as with the grammar checker—it can be ludicrously wrong in its observations. I keep it turned on, though, as its hit rate is good enough to make it worth watching.

I like to run the spelling checker just once, at the end of an edit or cleanup job, to catch things the naked eyeball missed plus any typos I inserted myself. Others prefer to run it twice, at the beginning and the end of a job, reducing the number of things to notice during the edit.

Run the spelling checker by pressing F7, then clicking the appropriate buttons in the dialog box (which tell Word to ignore the word flagged as an error; ignore all instances of that error; replace; and so on)—*after* you're sure what to do. For general vocabulary, if none of the suggestions are obviously and unquestionably what the file needs in place of what it already has, look up the word in the dictionary your client specified for the job before you allow any change to the file. And even if the word is valid, click "Add to Dictionary" only if it is something you know you'll want to accept as a general rule, not just on the current job.

Word 2010 has abandoned the spiffy trick in earlier versions that let you use "Ignore All" to take names out of play. (In Word 2003 and earlier versions, I would make sure to run the spelling checker on all the files for a book in one sitting, knowing that if it challenged any names that should already have been included, I had a consistency problem.) But it no longer remembers what you told it to ignore earlier in a given session; every file is a whole new game. As a result, you need to rely on your wetware memory for what should be showing up, or else use a separate custom dictionary to track names for each project.

> ***Stop-press news***: I just learned of a new wrinkle in the behavior of Word 2010. "Ignore All" is permanent. That is, once someone tells the spelling checker to ignore a word all the time, that word in that file will be ignored as long as the flag lasts - even if the file is transferred to another computer or saved under another name. I'm fairly sure this is post-2003 behavior - introduced as part of replacing the neat trick described in the preceding paragraph - but it escaped my notice until someone raised the issue on a discussion list late in 2013.
>
> You can get rid of any ignore-me flags left by your authors by telling Word to recheck each file when you run the spelling checker. The easiest way to do this is to press F7 to open the Spelling and Grammar dialog box and click Options at the lower left corner, which will take you straight to File, Options, Proofing. Click the "Recheck Document" box toward the lower left there, and Word will look at everything in the file (after which you can tell it to ignore what you want it to ignore).

Rearranging the Screen

Nothing's perfect. Even after you've got your screen environment—colors, typeface, spacing—set to the optimal values for your eyes and approach to the job, you'll still have places where you don't like what you see. It can be especially useful to compress lists and tables to get more of the text onto the screen at a time. To single-space a paragraph, press Ctrl+1 anywhere in it. You can select larger blocks of text and single-space them with the same built-in hot key. Use Ctrl+2 in the same way to double-space text.

If you're getting sleepy and can't afford to stop work for a break (which is what you should do if at all possible), changing the length of the lines or the size of the type will give you something refreshingly new to look at. To change the margins, press Ctrl+A to select the whole file, then go to the Page Setup group of the Page Layout ribbon. To change the apparent size of the type, use Alt+V, Z or the zoom slider in the lower right corner—or go to the Zoom group of the View ribbon. (The tip about using the "Show text wrapped within the document window" option, described under "Views" in chapter 2, comes in handy when you're playing with the zoom setting, as it will keep the text from slithering out of sight.) Switching from Draft view to Print Layout view or vice versa can also help you wake up.

The example in chapter 1 uses several tricks to get the citation list into a form that's easy to use. Select the whole thing, then shrink the type down to 9 point (plenty readable with Lucida Console, though I wouldn't recommend it for anything else); single-space the list, and then use Alt+O, C or the Columns icon on the Page Setup group of the Page Layout ribbon to make it use the scratch paper more efficiently.

✈ 3.c

4 Deploying the Custom Features

Word 2010 isn't limited to the things you get when you open the box, or even to the choices it offers on the various option dialogs. You can change almost everything about it fairly easily—the trick is finding out what's possible. This chapter talks about the features most likely to come in handy for an editor.

Once you've developed a set of custom features you like, you can take it with you when you change computers, and you can take most of it when you upgrade from one version of Word to another. It's not a one-step process, though—time was, copying your Normal template and your dictionaries would catch almost everything, but Word 2010 hides bits and pieces all over the place. The following discussions address ways of keeping each of your chosen features.

Exclusion Dictionary

As I say, Word can't read … but you can make it come close. That is, you can compensate for the biggest drawback of the spelling checker—its willingness to accept anything in its dictionary, no matter how embarrassing, that looks sort of like the word you meant to use—by giving it a set of words you always want it to challenge. My list (see Table 2: Hilary's Exclusion List) had eighty-nine words on it last time I looked at it, ranging from the unpreferred (such as "advisor"; my clients all want "adviser" instead) to the unbearable ("asses" in place of "assess," for instance). It's scary how many "mangers of pubic works" and "marital arts instructors" this technique has spared the world!

Word 2010 does a truly amazing job of hiding the procedures for setting up an exclusion dictionary. The "Check spelling and grammar" article in the Help system offers a link to an article promisingly titled "Use exclusion dictionaries to specify a preferred spelling for a word," but the link goes to a "page not available" screen if you're using only the Help files in your computer, and to a variety of articles—none on "trusted sites"—if you're online. You can follow the procedures that worked in earlier versions with no objection from Word 2010, but without getting an exclusion dictionary that it will actually use. (It took me two years to figure that one out!)

Instead, you need to find the empty file Word 2010 plans to use for an exclusion dictionary for your language and use a text editor to put your

Table 2: Hilary's Exclusion List

advisor	enrolment	miniscule
ameba	enrolments	minster
amidst	equalled	modelled
amongst	equalling	modelling
anus	florescent	mulinucleate
benefitted	focussed	Nurit
bestseller	focusses	plusses
bestsellers	focussing	polices
bestselling	fuelled	pollicies
busses	fuelling	posses
byproduct	fulfil	possiblity
byproducts	fulfiled	precisian
calvary	fulfils	prehumen
cancelled	gaol	pubic
canon	gong	publically
canons	impotent	scare
councillor	ism	skilful
councillors	landmine	supercede
counselled	landmines	theatre
counselling	likeable	tou
cueing	likeably	towards
cunt	MBWA	travelled
Danforth	McGowan	traveller
dependant	mange	travellers
dependants	manger	travelling
discus	mangers	umpping
discuses	marshalled	untied
enormity	marshalling	useable
enquiry	massage	whilst
enrol	mil	

chosen words into it. It will probably be in C:\Users\[your username]\AppData\Roaming\Microsoft\UProof. I copied the contents of MSSP3EN.exc (my Word 2003 exclusion dictionary) into ExcludeDictionaryEN0409.lex (the U.S. English exclusion dictionary, one of five versions for English I found on my system—along with one for French and one for Spanish—none of which had anything in them), and was back in the exclusion business. I found this procedure, which I heartily recommend, in an article titled "Create an Exclusion Dictionary" at http://wordfaqs.mvps.org/ExcludeWordFromDic.htm.

Your Own Keyboard

The stuff printed on the faces of the hundred-yumpty keys of your typical modern keyboard may seem like enough to keep track of, but Word comes out of the box with all sorts of other things hidden in various key combinations. It's a good idea to learn the ones for the things you do most often—especially Ctrl+C (copy), Ctrl+X (cut), and Ctrl+V (paste). The Insert Symbol dialog box (still available at Alt+I, S, but officially reached via "More Symbols" on the down-arrow at "Symbol" on the right side of the Insert ribbon) gives you the preprogrammed hot keys for special characters. And learn Ctrl+Z and Ctrl+Y—these are your basic get-out-of-trouble-free hot keys. The former will go back up Word's internal list of what you've done, one thing at a time, and wipe each one out as it gets to it; the latter will then go forward and put things back. Unfortunately, there's no way to skip anything in either direction; it's every step or none.

For a full list of the built-ins, point your browser to http://www.microsoft.com/enable/products/keyboard.aspx (http://tinyurl.com/BuiltInCombos) and click Word 2010 in the Office 2010 block of the table. (This charming site has the whole range of Microsoft shortcuts!) The function-key assignments are at the bottom of the list.

But there's more. Word really starts to fly when you put your own commands and choices on the keyboard, like the zippy little shortcut presented in the chapter 5 macro exercises that sticks a comma ahead of the next "and" in the file (so you can make a serial comma happen from three lines away instead of mousing to the spot) or the one in chapter 9 that turns a verb into a gerund.

The citation-checking example in chapter 1 makes use of three hot-key combos. Two are for macros (described later); the third repeats the Find Next command (Ctrl+PageDown). On my old keyboard, that was hard to reach, so I programmed Ctrl+Num0 (the zero on the number pad) to find the next instance of whatever I was looking for—in this case, an open paren. My new keyboard puts

→ 1.b

Ctrl+PageDown under my hand and makes the number pad a pain to deal with, so I'm back to vanilla on this tip.

At the moment, I have about fifty of these little jewels on my keyboard. How do I keep track? How do I even know how many there are? Simple: File, Print (still Alt+F, P), then click the down-arrow beside "Print All Pages" or type the letter A. That brings up a list of fascinating things you can print as well as (or instead of) the document you're looking at, including "Key Assignments," which sends your printer a list of all the tailored hot keys in Normal.dotm and other templates currently active on the system.

To assign a hot-key combination, go to File, Options, Customize Ribbon (Alt+T, O, C), and click the Customize button beside "Keyboard shortcuts" in the lower left corner (or repeat Alt+T at the end of the list earlier in this sentence). That opens the Customize Keyboard dialog box familiar from earlier versions of Word, where you can select a category (group of commands, macros, styles, or whatnot) in the panel on the left, then pick the item you want from the list on the right. Type the key combo you want to use in the "Press new shortcut key" box, then click Assign if it's safe—which it may not be.

> *Warning:* Most of the time, Word will tell you if your combo is already assigned to another task so you can decide if it's something you can afford to overwrite—but not always. Watch out for combos beginning with Alt; if you pair that key up with any of the letters that used to launch menus (File, Edit, View, Insert, fOrmat, Tools, tAble, Window, Help), Word will say "Yes, dear!" and reassign the combo, leaving you stuck with the ribbon to get to that function. (It's easy enough to delete the customization and thereby restore the original command when the problem surfaces, but I always feel like such a doofus when I forget….)

Controlling the Ribbon

Yes, you can puff up like a toad and declare the ribbon and all its works anathema, and as noted earlier, you can even buy products that will let you largely pretend that it doesn't exist. But the energy involved would be better spent getting to know the ribbon for yourself.

The stuff that Word used to put on toolbars and menus is mostly still there, lounging on the ribbon tabs or hiding in the undergrowth. The trick is to prowl around and find the bits you want. Figure 5 shows the ribbon configuration on my system as I write.

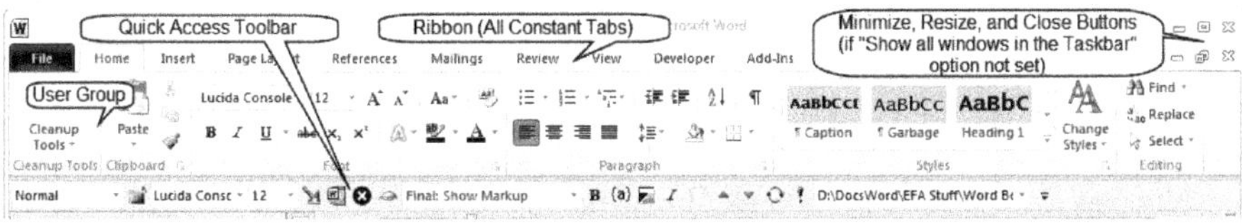

Figure 5. Close-Up of Hilary's Customized Interface

Start by going to "Customize Ribbon" (Alt+T, O, C) and setting the right column to All Tabs, then put a check mark beside everything—a lot of them won't show up unless you're in a place where you could use them, but they're good to have around and they don't get in the way. Their complete absence (which is what you get when they're unchecked) is just another instance of Microsoft's desire to protect you from straining your pretty little head, to which I say *pfui.*

Then take a few minutes really looking at each ribbon tab, considering what's there and what you wouldn't mind using that part of the ribbon to access. The groups make a fair amount of sense, and they have the advantage over the old menus of putting more functions out where you can see them. If you note things that you always want under your eye, put them on the QAT—and if you only *almost* always want them under your eye, stack them toward the left side of the Home ribbon, which is what's usually visible. And for things that you just want to do without looking for them, give them hot keys and ignore the ribbon thereafter.

I'm actually fairly unadventurous in my use of the ribbon. I haven't added anything of my own to it or removed anything from it. (But I did a quick test-drive when someone asked about customizing the ribbon or building a new tab while I was working on this book. I found that you can move tabs and groups around with the nifty little up and down nudge buttons on the Customize Ribbon screen [listed at Alt+T, O], and the ones farthest to the right are the first to shrink if there isn't room for all their bits. You can create tabs or groups from the same dialog. You can even remove groups entirely—which came as a surprise, as I recalled reading that some of the default stuff hangs on.) Here's a quick tour of what I do with the ribbon:

File tab. Not really a ribbon tab at all, File offers a variety of information and chores related to file management. It's essentially the old File menu expanded to fill the Word window, plus an Options list that resembles the one on the pre-2007 Tools menu (which I prefer to get to via Alt+T, O because it makes more sense to me than Alt, F, T). I use File mainly for printing, and for the recent-files list (Alt, F, R), which gives you hot keys for up to twenty-five recently opened files. (Specify how many you want to see at Alt+T, O, Advanced, Display.) File also replicates the pre-2007 Work menu by allowing you to pin specific files to the top of the list, so they stay there even if they'd otherwise get pushed down off it. And all the way at the bottom of the window, there's a little check box labeled "Quickly access this number of recent documents" beside a scroll box for a number; once you check and set that, you can type Alt+F to see the left pane of the File window display a list of files like the one on the pre-2007 File menu. If you've pinned that many files to the top of the list, it replicates the Work menu instead.

Home tab. Home more or less replicates the old Standard and Formatting toolbars, and is what the developers figured you'd want to see most often—so it's what you get with the ribbon expanded when you don't click on another tab. I've copied the bits I really want to the QAT or keyboard shortcuts, and I use it mainly for the highlighter color and the justification buttons. I haven't done anything to it, but one of my client templates installs itself there, and I've found it useful enough to keep.

Insert tab. I rarely look at Insert, except for the Symbols group and the Quick Parts item—and the latter is so complex that it needs a whole section of this chapter to itself.

Page Layout tab. Page Layout comes in handy for margins and columns.

References tab. I don't have much occasion to use the References tab, as the footnotes-and-endnotes dialog is still in my wetware memory as Alt+I, N, N. But there's lots of interesting stuff here—especially the Citations & Bibliography group, which certainly looks like it ought to be useful.

Mailings tab. Back when I was first installing Word 2010, I outfoxed myself and unchecked the Mailings tab entirely. No mass mailings in my work, no need for the tab, right? Wrongo. For some reason that doubtless made sense to the developers, all the commands for managing fields are lurking here, along with the settings for envelopes and labels.

Review tab. Just as I never used the Reviewing toolbar in pre-2007 editions of Word, I don't routinely use the Review tab in 2010. I open it mainly to get at the options that hide in the down-arrow on the Track Changes button (instead of being part of the main Options set, as in earlier versions of Word, where a rational human would look for them). I'd also use it for comparing documents, which never got enough use to ingrain the hot-key combo in my fingers.

View tab. There are easier ways to do everything on the View tab, mostly via Alt+V and the old View menu hot keys.

Developer tab. The Developer tab has the commands for using macros, add-ins, templates, and protection—but the ones I need I use from the keyboard. I sometimes contemplate this tab when I'm wondering about possibilities, but otherwise it stays out of sight.

Add-Ins tab. Add-Ins is where most of your extra tools and toolbars will show up. Once it's checked, it will appear when you get some add-in programs, such as Jack Lyon's FileCleaner (chapter 8), that don't create tabs of their own. If you upgrade from a pre-2007 version where you had your own user menus, they'll show up here—where they won't be nearly as convenient as they were. (It's rather like discovering your refrigerator has been moved out to the garage, rather than sitting in the kitchen.) I switched all of mine over to macros that offer choices; you'll get samples if you download the files for the exercises in chapter 5.

> *Note:* Contrary to what was my fond expectation and may well be yours, your ribbon customizations are not saved in your Normal template. See the next section, "QAT and Carry," for tips on moving or preserving them.

QAT and Carry

Like the ribbon customizations, the Quick Access Toolbar does not live in Normal.dotm. This is good, as it saves these crucial parts of your environment from the constant risk of corruption that the Normal template suffers. But it's an awful shock when you carry your prized template to a new computer and your carefully constructed QAT and ribbon don't show up to welcome you. (I learned this the hard way, demonstrating Word 2010 to a room-filling workshop a month or so after I'd started using the program.)

To copy your QAT and ribbon so you can use them elsewhere (or as a backup in case something awful happens to your computer), press Alt+T, O, C, Alt+P to get to the import and export dropdown menu on the Customize Ribbon dialog. (There's another button for it on the Quick Access Toolbar section of the Options dialog, but it does the same thing.) Click "Export all customizations" and put the .exportedUI file where you can find it again.

Importing a customization file overwrites any customizations already in place on a computer, and there's no backup. So if you're going to be working temporarily on somebody else's computer, remember to export the current settings before you import your own—it's not friendly to go into someone's house and rearrange the furniture!

> *Note:* The import and export function should do the job for you, without reference to the actual QAT and ribbon files. However, if you decide you need them, Windows XP stores them at C:\Documents and Settings\[your username]\Local Settings\Application Data\Microsoft\Office. Windows 7 puts them at C:\Users\[your username]\AppData\Local\Microsoft\Office.

AutoText and Quick Parts

AutoText used to be part of the AutoCorrect family, but it's now under a new feature called Quick Parts, in the Text group of the Insert ribbon. AutoText entries can be substantially longer than AutoCorrect entries, and they can include all sorts of formatting. For instance, the airplane tip boxes in this book are all based on a master stored in my AutoText collection.

You can put your AutoText collection into a template file—I started out with one cleverly called "OldAutotext.dotx"—in which case it will work just as it always did: when you type the first four letters of a trigger, you should see an AutoComplete tooltip notifying you that you can get the full text if you press Enter from that point on. If you keep typing past the end of the trigger, you get what you type, without the conversion. If you take this approach, however, you have to arrange to load that template every time you run Word, either by putting it in the Startup directory or by checking it off on the list of global templates (still available by pressing Alt+T, I).

Alternatively, you can turn your AutoText items into what Word now calls Building Blocks, which puts them where the program expects to find them. Doing so costs you the nifty four-letter trigger; you have to press F3 to activate an AutoText Building Block—but at least you only have to type the first few letters of the trigger phrase.

> *Tale of Woe and Intrigue*: I found out about the F3 problem after moving my whole collection into the Building Blocks gallery. Had I Only Known, I'da kept hands off—especially since moving them from the old AutoText template to the Building Blocks gallery invalidated the old template, so it wouldn't work even when loaded as global. However, I found a clean copy of the old AutoText template on my travel computer and copied it over the one I'd wrecked, and that put me back in the AutoText AutoComplete biz ... some of the time. These days, if I type in an AutoText trigger and

> get the AutoComplete tooltip, pressing Enter will give me the full item; if I don't get the tooltip, pressing Enter will give me a hard return—but pressing F3 will give me the item. I'm getting the tooltips perhaps 25 percent of the time, just enough to be truly frustrating. Experience says, if you haven't poisoned your AutoText collection, don't.

Creating new AutoText items or Building Blocks is easy: Just select the material you want to use, then press Alt+F3. Alternatively, you can click the down-arrow beside Quick Parts on the Insert ribbon and choose "Save Selection to Quick Part Gallery," or type Alt, N, Q, S to get to the same dialog box Alt+F3 gives you. Then follow the prompts there to name and define the material so you can get back to it. You can use the "Save in" line to send the item to whatever template you're using for AutoText.

You can print a list of AutoText entries straight from Word—just press Alt+F, P, A to activate the down-arrow beside the default "Print All Pages" setting, and then select "AutoText Entries" instead to send a list to the printer.

The "standard queries" described in the citation-checking process in chapter 1 all make use of AutoText entries in a client-specific query shell (see "Templates" in chapter 5). Here are some of my AutoText triggers and their corresponding stored phrases:

→ 4.b(3-5)

- *noref:* The Reference section lacks an entry for this citation. Please supply.
- *nocite:* There appears to be no citation to this source in the text. Please either insert one or delete the reference.
- *badname:* This author's name is spelled differently in text and Reference section. Please fix as needed.
- *baddate:* The only similar reference has a different date—please adjust as needed.

It's useful to keep AutoText entries fairly generic, then edit them as needed. My "badname" text often gets changed after I invoke it—for example, to "The second author's name is spelled differently in text and Reference section. Please fix as needed."

A Matter of Style

If you're working primarily with semantic content and not with appearance, the easiest way to deal with something that looks funny is to kill all the formatting and reapply what it's supposed to have:

- To get rid of character-level formatting such as italics, select the offending text and press Ctrl+[space]. That restores the text to the basic provisions of the style attached to the paragraph.
- To get rid of paragraph-level formatting applied on top of a paragraph style, place the cursor anywhere in the paragraph and press Ctrl+Q. For example, if you find a paragraph with extra line spacing, press Ctrl+Q to revert to the standard spacing for that style.
- To get rid of the paragraph style entirely, press Ctrl+Shift+N from anywhere in the paragraph. That almost always reassigns the Normal style, eliminating any paragraph-level style that may have been applied.

If a style refuses to convert to Normal—and for some reason, "Normal (Web)" is a big offender, but it's not alone—go to the Styles dialog (press Ctrl+Alt+Shift+S), mouse over the style you want to get rid of, and click the down-arrow that appears beside it to get the option to delete it. Once it's gone, the text it was clutching will revert to Normal. Figure 6 shows the Styles list, so you can tell you've gotten to the right place.

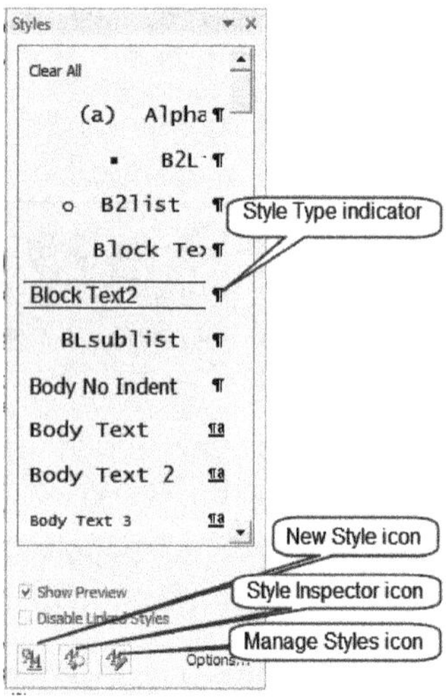

Figure 6. The Styles Dialog

There's a free add-in called CrossEyes that provides a Reveal Codes function for Word and comes remarkably close to the one mourned by former WordPerfect users. It shows you the file contents with flags for the beginning and end of character styles and other elements next to the text they apply to, even though Word is actually putting them in the part of the file that shows on screen as the pilcrow at the end of the paragraph, section, or file. See chapter 8 for more info on this application.

If you need to work with styles rather than around them, the least intrusive trick is to keep the Apply Styles floating dialog visible all the time. (Press Ctrl+Shift+S to turn it on [see Figure 7]. If you get a pane at the left side of the screen instead of the neat little box shown in the figure, place the pointer in the title bar and drag it outside the Word window.) If you check the AutoComplete box, the Style Name text box will let you select a style by typing the first few

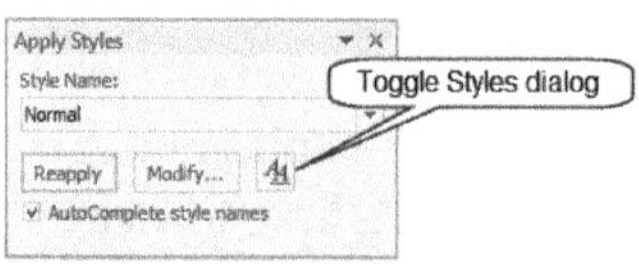

Figure 7. Apply Styles Box

letters of the name. The Reapply and Modify buttons are self-explanatory, and the double-A icon toggles the Styles dialog (see Figure 6) on and off.

> *Tip*: Mousing over a style name on the Styles dialog also opens a box that details the style's properties. The double-A-plus-pencil icon at the bottom of the Styles dialog box list takes you to the pre-2007 dialog for managing styles.

Voice Controls: Look, Ma, No Hands!

Word 2010 lacks the speech engine that came with Word 2002+, leaving that function to the operating system—which acquired it with Windows Vista. So I was out of luck for years, until I upgraded from XP to Windows 7 in 2012. Now I'm back in the voice biz in a small way; every once in a while, something seems easier to say than to type, but I'm really out of the habit. When my old desktop microphone wouldn't work with Windows 7, I managed to flange a USB headset into the same holder—looking yet more like Rube Goldberg on an off day—so I still don't have to wear the thing.

You can find instructions for setting up and using speech recognition on the Microsoft website, at http://office.microsoft.com/en-us/word-help/what-happened-to-speech-recognition-HA010369151.aspx?CTT=1 (http://tinyurl.com/newspeech).

Under the new system, you can use your voice to control the keyboard, which puts the most useful commands—especially "Page Up" and "Page Down"—in easy reach. You can activate the Alt key to get to the items on the QAT, say "Press Alt F8" to get to the list of active macros and talk your way to the one you want, or recite your hot-key combinations to run the macros you've attached to them.

5 Macros and Templates

Macros and templates are at the absolute heart of making Word 2010 your own. Anything you do repetitively is quicker and easier to do with a macro, and anything you see is controlled by a template whether you are deliberately using one or not. If you want to pick up editing speed without sacrificing quality, you *need* your own macros and templates—and it really isn't all that complex or difficult to wrap your mind around them.

All the files for this chapter are on my website, at http://www.powersedit.com/ftp/Word2010exercises.zip.

If you download and unzip that archive, you'll find the exercises much easier to follow—and you'll need some of the files for the exercises in the "Templates" section of this chapter. As a bonus, the archive also includes a file with the text of the macros in chapter 9, so you won't have to type those in if you want to play with them, and another file with the text of the sample style sheet discussed in chapter 10 and shown in Figure 12.

Macros

A macro is a way of storing a bunch of instructions for your computer, so you can get the effect you want by asking for it rather than going through all the steps. It's sort of like the difference between phoning for a pizza and digging out all the ingredients and the baking stone to make your own, but with the advantage that what you get is your own recipe and not Pizza Hut's; you just don't have to do the work. And you don't have to be a programmer to use macros: simply learn how to record them and then how to get at them. It also helps to learn how to pick up macros others have written and use them on your computer—and for a real sense of control, learn how to read them and make simple adjustments.

None of that crosses the line into programming. And as long as you keep your macros in Normal.dotm or a separate macro template, none of it is in any way detectable by your clients. The macros you use do not travel with your .docx files; you'd have to make special .docm files for that—and why bother? It'd just scare people.

Sample Applications

For sheer joyous jollies, here are the macros I use most often, and what I use them for:

SerialAnd: Inserts a comma before the next instance of the word "and," so I can put in a serial comma as soon as I notice I'll need it, usually about three or four lines ahead of the cursor. (The exercises in this chapter will lead you through building your own copy of this jewel—and its companion, SerialOr.)

Ingydingy: Changes the end of the current word to "ing"—"cruised" to "cruising," for example.

Hyphenate: Deletes the space between two words and replaces it with a hyphen.

CutPaste: Deletes selected text and pastes it back in, to consolidate a bunch of tracked changes.

StyleThat and *HedOnBack*: One copies selected words to the style sheet, and the other puts a new line there, returns to the edit document, and clears the selection. (I want to stop on the style sheet so as to add the part of speech or make other adjustments before going on with the edit.)

A0APlainStyle: Attaches my favorite styles template, turns on Track Changes, and sets the zoom factor to 85%.

BookCodez: Offers a list of coding choices, then does whichever one I select.

Nothing complex in that list, and nothing that could be twisted to damage my computer—but every single one saves seconds, and it's amazing how fast seconds add up to hours.

To go into more detail, the citation-checking example in chapter 1 makes use of two macros—the ones called "Fillerup" and "GetThat" in chapter 9—for each citation. The first one starts at the cursor and selects everything through the next closing parenthesis—allowing you to pick up authors' names whether they're inside the parens with the date or not. The second takes the selected text, copies it to another document (I use the end of the style sheet for this), moves to a new line there, returns to the main document, finds the next open parenthesis, and stops immediately to its right. If that turns out to be the beginning of a citation, all I have to do is hit the Fillerup combo again, followed by the GetThat combo—respectively Ctrl+Shift+[semicolon] and Ctrl+[semicolon] on my system. Otherwise, I either move the cursor to the real beginning and proceed as before, or press Ctrl+PageDown for Find Next.

→ 1.b

Guided Practice with Macros

Working through the steps that follow will take you from a simple introductory macro to fairly giddy heights in a couple of hours. You can work with a scratch file of your own and type in the sample macro if you prefer, but to save steps and be sure of seeing exactly what the exercises describe, I recommend working on the garbage file and with the macro in the archive described at the beginning of the chapter.

Word 2010 includes a variety of tools for getting any given effect: if you don't like mousing to the ribbon, you can use the built-in hot keys; if you don't like the ribbon hot keys, you can use the ones for the departed menus. However, for these exercises, I strip it back to the bone and present things one way most of the time—not the only way, but one that will work if you take a literal-minded approach to doing exactly what it says.

When you're done with the three exercises, you'll have all the mental tools you need to make and borrow macros for your own work.

> *Safety tip*: It's no accident that these exercises have you working on a garbage file. To be safe, don't build macros in the middle of a live file. Instead, pick up a few pages out of a project that you want to develop a macro for and work on those until you're satisfied that it's doing what you want and nothing else. And save even a garbage file before you run a new version of your macro on it; that way you have a clean copy to return to and won't have to sit there pressing Ctrl+Z for every step of the macro if it goes wrong.

Setup

If you've been reading along without trying the recommended settings, hold off on these exercises until you've gone through the following preliminaries:

1. *Start Word and open WordWork.docx.*
    a. Press Ctrl+O to start Word's File, Open dialog.
    b. Navigate to the directory where you put WordWork.docx.
    c. Highlight the file name and double-click it.
2. *Make sure the ribbon includes what you need.*
    a. Press Alt+T, O (or go to Options on the File tab) and click Customize Ribbon.
    b. In the right column, check the Developer tab.

3. *Get access to other good stuff.*

   a. If you don't see the macro recorder icon on the Word Status bar (it looks like a miniature window with a red dot in the upper left corner), right-click anywhere on the bar and check the box for it on the Customize Status Bar list. While you're there, click everything else, too—there's probably room, and most of it comes in handy.

   b. Press Alt+T, O, D to get to the Display options, and check "Show document tooltips on hover."

   c. Go to the Trust Center (Alt+T, O, T) and click Trust Center Settings, ignoring the warning not to mess with them. Under Trusted Locations, make sure your template directories are listed. Windows 7 users will probably find them at C:\Users\[your username]\AppData\Roaming\Microsoft\Templates and C:\Users\[your username]\AppData\Roaming\Microsoft\Word\STARTUP. Windows XP users will probably find them at C:\Documents and Settings\[your username]\Application Data\Microsoft\Templates and C:\Documents and Settings\[your user name]\Application Data\Microsoft\Word\Startup. Under Macro Settings, check "Trust access to the VBA project object model." Select the third radio button ("Disable all macros except digitally signed macros"), which should allow your own macros—and macros you've made your own—to run. While you're in the Trust Center Settings, look at the Privacy Options and uncheck "Warn before printing, saving or sending a file that contains tracked changes or comments" if you're tired of Word repeatedly asking if you really want to save your edits.

Macronipulation

The best way to take possession of the concept of using macros is to make and use one, so start here. This exercise is a variant on "Hello, World!"—the traditional first step in exploring any computer control system. In it, you type a phrase in plain text and put one of the words in boldface, and then have the mild pleasure of watching your computer type it back at you. The effort is harmless but not pointless; it gives you some safe experience (and incidentally generates some code that will come in handy in a later exercise).

1. *Record a macro.*

   a. Press Ctrl+End to get to the bottom of the WordWork.docx file.

b. Click the macro recorder icon in the Word Status bar. (If your screen is too narrow to show the icon, go to the Developer tab on the ribbon and click Record Macro in the Code group at the far left.)

c. Type "x" in the Macro Name box that appears, then press Enter. (Ignore everything else in the dialog.)

d. Type "What? Me make friends with Word?!" and press Enter.

e. Press Ctrl+[Up Arrow] to move the cursor to the beginning of the line you just typed.

f. Press Ctrl+[Right Arrow] four times to move the cursor to the beginning of "friends."

g. Press Ctrl+Shift+[Right Arrow] to select "friends" and the following space.

h. Press Shift+[Left Arrow] to unselect the space.

i. Press Ctrl+B to put "friends" in boldface.

j. Press End to move the cursor to the end of the line, then press Enter to finish the paragraph and move to the next line.

k. Click the macro recorder icon—which has lost its red dot—again to stop recording. (Or click Stop Recording on the Developer tab.)

2. *Play your macro.*

   a. Press Alt+F8. (This opens the macro dialog, also found at Developer, Macros.)

   b. Highlight "x" on the list of macro names. (Notice how the name appears on the Macro Name line when you highlight it. If you already have too many macros for "x" to be visible in the box, just type it in on the Macro Name line, then press [Down Arrow] until the name "x" is highlighted if it hasn't leapt into sight. This works for any macro name—just start typing and the list will scroll toward it, allowing you to use the [Down Arrow] key to select it as soon as you see it.)

   c. Press Enter. Watch your screen do your work again.

3. *Assign your macro to a hot key.*

   a. Press Alt+T, O, C, Alt+T. (This opens Word 2010's version of the Customize Keyboard dialog box, which looks exactly like the one you may be used to from earlier versions. Keep the default "Save changes in" setting, Normal.dotm.)

b. Press M twice to get to your macros. (Huh what? Dial M for Macro? You can't tell by looking at it, but when you open the Customize Keyboard dialog box, the "Categories" list is active and awaiting your input. Any letter you type will take you to a list item beginning with that letter, and if you don't like the one you get, pressing the same letter again will give you the next possibility. So the first time you press M the list will jump to "Mailings Tab," and the second time it will jump to "Macros.")

c. Click in the Macros list (on the right side of the box) to switch the computer's attention there, and then press X to highlight "x."

d. Type a hot-key combo in the "Press new shortcut key" box. (Make sure it is not already assigned to something you want to keep. WARNING: Be careful not to double up on the gone-but-not-forgotten Menu bar hot keys—Alt+A for Table, Alt+I for Insert, Alt+O for Format, Alt+T for Tools, and the rest—as Word won't warn you before you reuse them. If you forget, just unassign your error—highlight it on the Current keys list and click Remove—and it will go back to its proper home without further work.)

e. Click Assign, then Close. Close the Customize dialog.

f. Press your hot key. Here comes that idiot statement again....

4. *Set up a QAT button for testing macros.* As with any other piece of writing, the first draft of a macro probably won't be perfect. But unlike your usual text, problems in a macro are apt to escape your editorial eye; you find out what's wrong by watching it (fail to) work. This trick gives you one-click access to your macro-in-progress from the Word screen, where you can see what happens.

a. Press Alt+T, O, Q to get the customize dialog box for the Quick Access Toolbar (QAT).

b. Click the down-arrow in the "Choose commands from" dialog box, then highlight "Macros" in the list that opens. (Pressing M works here, too.)

c. Highlight "Normal.NewMacros.x" on the list of macros and click Add in the center of the dialog box.

d. Use the up-arrow and down-arrow beside the right column to move your macro to the relative position you prefer. (I like it out in the middle somewhere.)

e. Click "Modify" below the column and select an icon that makes sense to you. (I prefer the bright red circle with a white X in the middle, but any icon will work as long as it's something you can remember. Left to itself, Word will use the same icon for all your macros—and that way lies madness.)

f. Press Esc to close the dialog box.

g. Click the button to exercise your macro. Yup; it still does the same thing. (Keep this button! As long as you call every macro you record or build "x" until you're happy enough to give it a name and store it away, you'll be able to use this button to test whatever macro you happen to be working on.)

Macropropriation

I make and use macros all the time, but freely admit that I'm not a VBA wonk and know little about how the system really works. Instead, I'm an enthusiastic scavenger. I love finding macros that do useful things and hanging them on my system. In addition, I can read VBA code just well enough to figure out what a line is doing and tweak it to make it do something similar, and that's pretty much all an editor needs. In this exercise, you pick up a basic serial-comma-inserting macro and get it working on your computer.

1. *Copy a macro.*

   a. Go to the end of the WordWork.docx file.

   b. Select all the text under the "Found Macro" heading, from "Sub" through "End Sub."

   c. Press Ctrl+C to copy the macro. Alternatively, if you want to do it the hard way, type the following text exactly as shown (including the straight single and double quote marks) into a new document, and copy that.

```
Sub SerialAnd()
' Macro written 02/27/03 by Hilary Powers
' Inserts a comma after the next instance of
' the word "and" following the cursor.
' Use when you see you need to add a serial comma.
    Selection.Find.ClearFormatting
```

```
        With Selection.Find
                .text = "and"
                .MatchCase = True
                .MatchWholeWord = True
                .Forward = True
                .Wrap = wdFindStop
        End With
        Selection.Find.Execute
        Selection.MoveLeft Unit:=wdCharacter, Count:=2
        Selection.TypeText text:=","
End Sub
```

2. *Start the macro editor.*

   a. Press Alt+F11 to open the VBA editor. You should see a window with two narrow panels stacked down the left side, a large gray area, and a Title bar that says "Microsoft Visual Basic for Applications," along with the name of the current active file in Word. (Figure 8 shows a sample, open to the ClientBase template used later in this chapter.)

   b. The first time you press Alt+F11, you may get a bare-bones window without the narrow side panels. If that happens, go to the window's View menu and click Project Explorer, then go back to the View menu and click Properties Window. Resize the panels to take up about equal amounts of space, one below the other, in a strip about two and a half inches wide against the left margin of the window. (They should stay open from here on out, but this procedure will get them back if they do disappear.)

3. *Paste the copied macro into NewMacros.*

   a. In the Project window (the one in the upper left), double-click NewMacros under "Normal." (You may need to click the plus sign beside "Normal" and then the one beside "Modules" to see it.)

   b. Move the pointer to the end of the NewMacros section that appears in the Code window (the large area at the right). You should see the text of the "x" macro you just recorded at the end of the list of macros—and it may well be the only thing there. (If you've never played with macros, you probably didn't even have a NewMacros module until you recorded "x"; Word creates the module only when called for.)

   c. Press Ctrl+V to paste in the text of the macro below "End Sub."

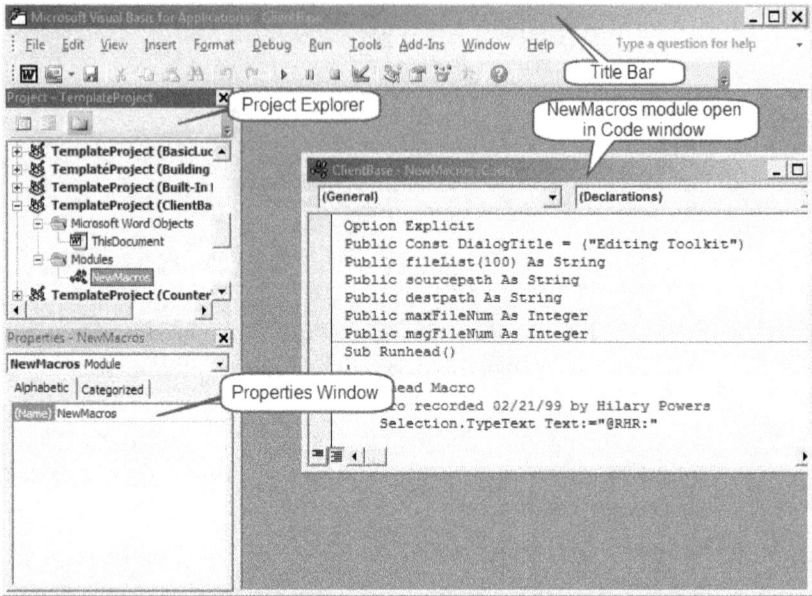

Figure 8. VBA Editor Window

4. *Set up to use your new macro.*
   a. Return to Word. (You can just click the Word icon on the Windows Taskbar.) WordWork.docx should still be open.
   b. Move the cursor to the first paragraph after "Second-Level Head."
   c. Click "Track Changes:" on the Word Status bar to turn on change tracking.
5. *Run your macro from the VBA editor.*
   a. Make sure that WordWork.docx is the only document that's open.
   b. Return to the VBA editor via the Windows Taskbar.
   c. Move the cursor into the new macro.
   d. With the macro name showing in the small box at the top right of the Code window (the one that says "Declarations" in the figure), press F5.
   e. Return to Word and see the results.

f. Press Ctrl+[Right Arrow] twice to move the cursor past the word "and."

6. *Macronipulate*: Play your macro again from the list at Alt+F8, then give it a hot key of its own. If you need hints:

   a. Press Alt+F8 and then press S to get you near the new macro name, SerialAnd. Select it and click Run.

   b. Open the Customize Keyboard dialog box (Alt+T, O, C, Alt+T), press M twice to get to the Macros category, and find SerialAnd on the list of macros. Either use the same hot key as before (you can change it later), or assign a new one.

Macroreconstruction

The serial-comma macro you've been playing with is already fairly useful; it saves you the trouble of mousing to the next "and" when you perceive that it's going to need a comma. But it's not as useful as it could be. Trigger it twice in a row without moving the cursor, and you get two commas in a row—not something you're ever likely to want. It'd be much better if it took the initiative and moved away from the spot it just found, so that if you're dealing with a sentence that has three separate lists in it—which I've seen, sometimes repeatedly and in edits too light to support rewriting—you can simply trigger it three times and go your way rejoicing.

1. *Return to the VBA editor via the Windows Taskbar.*

2. *Collect a command to cannibalize.*

   a. Read through the "x" macro in the VBA Code window.

   b. Select the whole line that reads "Selection.MoveRight Unit:= wdWord, Count:=4" and press Ctrl+C.

3. *Fix the macro.*

   a. Go to the SerialAnd macro.

   b. Place the cursor at the beginning of the "End Sub" line and press Ctrl+V, and then press Enter.

   c. Change the "Count:=[number]" at the end of the new line from 4 to 2.

4. *Observe the macro's new behavior.*

   a. Return to Word via the Windows Taskbar.

b. Move the cursor up to the beginning of the third paragraph after "Second-Level Head."

c. Run the macro twice in succession from the hot key or dialog. Note that you no longer need to move the cursor by hand after each use.

5. *Build a new tool.*

a. Return to the VBA editor via the Windows Taskbar.

b. Copy the entire revised SerialAnd macro, from "Sub" through "End Sub."

c. Move to the end of the "End Sub" line, press Enter, and then paste in your copy of the macro.

d. Replace "and" with "or" in the macro title, comments, and "text =" line.

e. Return to Word and give SerialOr its own hot key.

f. Try it out in WordWork.docx, starting at the beginning of the second paragraph after "Second-Level Head."

Macro Tips and Tricks

If you've been following along, your fingers already know enough about macros to do almost all of what you'll need. Nonetheless, things will go more smoothly with a bit more info about the environment and its hidden gotchas. (The headings in this section follow the pattern set in a grimoire attributed to Albertus Magnus; Word reminds me of ceremonial magic, and if that's what it is, these are cantrips.)

To Take Advantage of the Macro Editor Screen

I skipped rapidly over the VBA screen earlier, but knowing a little more will make it easier to get along. (Look back at Figure 8 if you're reading without the screen in front of you.)

Get used to the Project Explorer (the little panel with a title bar saying "Project – [something else; probably either 'TemplateProject' or 'Normal']" at the left side of the screen)—that's the VBA editor's directory. It shows all the items active at the moment, and you're apt to need it a lot. Each of the boldface stubs (Normal, for instance) designates a template or document, and the plus sign beside it is a promise of stuff inside. If you click the one by Normal, it will open to "Microsoft Word Objects" and "Modules"; ignore the former and double-click the latter, and you'll get to "NewMacros," which is what you want.

Active global templates (discussed later in this chapter; you may not have any now, but I see fifteen of them here) will show up as boldface stubs on the list, but will refuse to open when clicked unless you open them as files in Word first. Word will happily let you have a template open as a .dotm file while you work with the macros in it; in fact, it will insist for anything but Normal.dotm.

Directly below the Project Explorer is the Properties window, which includes much strange stuff of interest to real VBA wonks. Don't worry about it until and unless you get into serious macro creation.

The main action is in the Code window, which is the VBA editor's work surface. You can stack NewMacros modules and individual macros from different templates there. Rather than letting a macro or module take up the whole Code window, it's useful to keep them at about a quarter of the available space, so that you can stack them with their Title bars showing and skip back and forth easily. If you really need to see more of a given macro, click the full-screen icon in the top right corner (the one shaped like a little screen). That will let it fill the Code window—but it won't eat the rest of the monitor. Click the resize icon (what the full-screen one turned into; it now looks like two little screens) when you're through with the chore that needed the space.

Take some time to go over the menus and toolbar buttons. The controls are remarkably self-explanatory when you get into them. (The VBA editor is still ribbon-free.)

And if you need more help, it's actually available there in unusual quantity and quality. Help on the VBA window's Menu bar opens up an index of useful stuff. And when you're working on a macro, right-clicking on a bit of code can produce some remarkably apt context-sensitive advice.

In addition, the VBA editor has another helpful trick that will come in handy if you ever move beyond revising macros and into writing them: it will often tell you what's acceptable to write next. (This is programming, so feel free to ignore this paragraph if you don't want to go there.) VBA text tends to put words together into strings in a quite Germanic fashion, separating parts of a string with periods instead of spaces—as in the first line of the "SerialAnd" macro: Selection.Find.ClearFormatting. If you type in the first part of such a

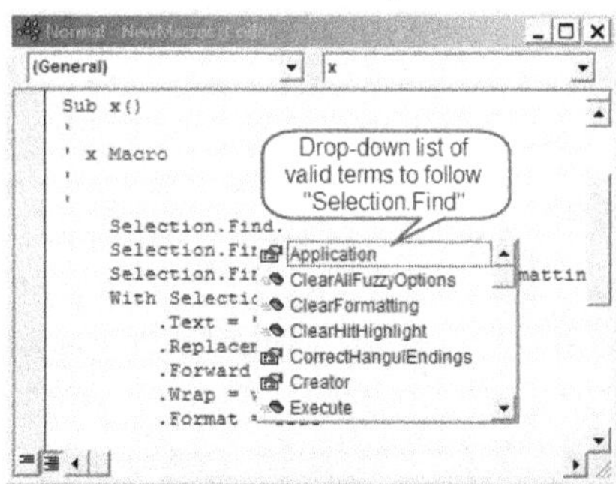

Figure 9. VBA Code Suggestions

string followed by a period (say, "Selection."), Word will give you a list of the things that would be valid to put next. Select one of those, let Word put it in, and type another period—and you'll get another list of what might go next (see Figure 9). And if you select a string (or partial string) and press F1, VBA Help will kick in and quite possibly tell you enough to let you figure out if you're on the right track.

To Record a Macro Easily

Practice the moves you intend to record until you're sure you can do them smoothly. When you're ready, click the macro recorder icon on the Status bar, then follow the prompts.

As noted earlier, it's best to give all recorded macros the same name—I use "x"—and rename them after they're working properly. (That way, you don't wind up with a gazillion macros that never quite did what you wanted, mixed up with fragments of code you recorded because you wanted to stuff them into other macros.) When you give "x" a permanent name, remember that it has to be one word (like the macros in chapter 9)—no spaces allowed.

Further recording tips, from correspondence with uber-editor Dan Wilson of The Editor's DeskTop:

- If you need to use Find or Replace in the macro, get set up before you start recording. That is, press Ctrl+H to open the dialog box, click More if you see it, and empty the text and options boxes. Make sure "All" is selected from the Search direction drop-down menu, then close the dialog box and begin recording.
- If you need to use any dialog box in the macro (including Find and Replace), open it after you start recording. If you need to use more than one tab of a dialog box, close the dialog box after the first tab. Then reopen it, click the tab you need next and use it, close the dialog box again, and so on.
- Remember that you can use the mouse to select menu commands but not to select text. Use F8 to select text: Click to place the cursor where you want it—the recorder will ignore you—then press F8 twice to select a word, thrice to select a sentence, four times to select a paragraph, five to select a section of the document, and six to select the whole thing. You can also select text by pressing Shift (and Ctrl if you need it), along with the arrow keys.

To Remember Why

In a macro, a single straight quote mark designates the rest of the line as something for humans rather than computers to read. These "comments" are vastly useful as your macro collection increases: they help you remember where things come from and what they do, which doubtless seem as clear as the current date when you install the macro—and will be as hard to remember months or years later when you look through the collection and try to figure out what does what. For a long macro that makes good use of comments, see "Converting Any Integer to Text" in chapter 9.

Comments come in handy when you want a macro to ignore part of its instructions for a given run. Just put a single quote mark at the beginning of any line you don't want to use this time. See the "Coding Running Heads" section of chapter 9 for a macro that includes samples of commented-out commands.

To Run a Macro inside a Macro

It's often convenient to take a bit of code that does a simple chore and have other macros use it without copying it in. And it's dead simple—just add a line that says "Call [othermacroname]" wherever you want to do what that macro says. Put in the name of the macro you want to use, but without the empty parens () at the end. For example, if you put the following code into the template with your other macros, you can add "Call ClearFindAndReplaceParameters" after the Sub line of any macro that uses a Find and Replace operation—SerialAnd, for instance—and be sure it will run normally even if you've been using some of the special options, like wildcards, that would otherwise screw it up.

```
Sub ClearFindAndReplaceParameters()
' Utility Code provided 4-1-08
' by David Chinell of Word-PC
With Selection.Find
   .ClearFormatting
   .Replacement.ClearFormatting
   .text = ""
   .Replacement.text = ""
   .Forward = True
   .Wrap = wdFindStop
   .Format = False
   .MatchCase = False
   .MatchWholeWord = False
   .MatchWildcards = False
   .MatchSoundsLike = False
   .MatchAllWordForms = False
End With
End Sub
```

Templates

Word 2010 still uses a separate file called a "template" to govern its operations. If you don't tell it to use something else, what you get is a template called "Normal.dotm," which provides a generic set of styles and formatting information and sets up a basic environment for you. (In pre-2007 versions of Word, that meant that if you wanted Computer B to act like Computer A, copying Normal.dot from A to B would do the job for you. That's no longer the case; you still need to copy Normal.dotm, but it won't give you your ribbon and QAT customizations. See "QAT and Carry" in chapter 4 for the procedure for moving ribbon and QAT customizations.) If you want anything different—your own AutoText and hot keys, your own default page layout, your own choice of fonts and styles—you either change Normal or build a new template, or you do some of both.

Updating Normal is both the easiest and the riskiest course of action. It's easiest because every new style definition, hot key, and recorded macro defaults to Normal; it takes additional steps to make something go anywhere else. But because Normal is always grinding along in the background, it's exposed to random damage—making it virtually certain to turn toes-up some day, at which point Word will stop working properly. Its constant use also makes it a preferred target of virus writers. If (when) it goes out of action, it's not the end of the world; all you have to do is close Word, delete or rename Normal.dotm, and restart. Word will create a nice new all-default Normal for you, and you'll be back in business ... without your customizations. (See "Simple Insanity" in chapter 7 for more on digging out of Word trouble; regenerating Normal life is just one of several possibilities, and not the first one to try.)

Besides Normal, Word offers several choices for templates:

- Attached to files or loaded as global. Attached templates travel with the files, whereas global templates affect only your own computer and only when they're active.
- If global, loaded automatically when you start Word or selected for a given session or operation. Templates in Word's Startup directory are active every time Word starts; aside from Normal, the templates in Word's regular template directory are active only when you request them via the lower half of the Templates and Add-Ins dialog.
- Including macros or not (indicated by file types .dotm and .dotx). Common security settings may cause client systems to restrict files attached to templates that include macros, so it's useful to keep your macros in your own sandbox.

All of these choices can be either good or bad, depending on the particular situation—and there's no one best way. The following sections describe the approach I've worked out.

Using Templates

I take a mixed approach to the use of templates. For basic style and formatting decisions in my own documents, I go ahead and allow Normal to update. (At Alt+T, O, Advanced, Save, there's a check box that requires Word to ask before saving the Normal template. If it's checked, Word will ask about saving Normal next time you save or close the file you're working on; otherwise it'll just do it. I go back and forth on this, as it's a malware protection to have Word ask before saving the template … but some add-ins and other things change it in imperceptible and harmless ways, so that checking the ask-before-saving box can lead to almost constant message boxes.) Whenever I change Normal.dotm—or, to be honest, whenever I notice that I've done so—I make a copy: go to File, Open and point to the directory where the templates are kept—which should be the top item on the look-in list at the left side of the dialog (at least I've never heard from anyone who didn't find it there). Double-click Normal.dotm—which opens happily even though it's in use—and save a copy: Press F12 to get to File, Save As, and name the file NormBakMMDDYY.dotm (where "MMDDYY" represents the day's date).

In case you need to hunt for it, the real Windows 7 address will be C:\Users\[your username]\AppData\Roaming\Microsoft\Templates, unless your copy of Word has been given special instructions. Windows XP will use C:\Documents and Settings\[your username]\Application Data\Microsoft\Templates. If you can't find this path on your computer, go to the Windows Control Panel and click Folder Options, View (in the Appearance and Personalization section if you're using the category view), and set the "Show hidden files and folders" radio button to on. While you're there, it's also a good idea to uncheck "Hide extensions for known file types." Earlier versions of Word didn't actually care where you kept your templates, and I used to keep both regular templates and the ones in Startup on the data disk (on my computer, a different physical component from the one with the programs). It's a hassle to do that in Word 2010, however, and I've given up on the practice since upgrading.

I keep several editions of Normal, so I can always go back to a good copy. If I have to kill it, rather than let Word build me a new one, I simply delete or rename the bad Normal.dotm, copy the most recent backup in Windows

Explorer, name it Normal.dotm, and go on my way—and if that one doesn't work for some reason, I can go back to an earlier version.

For the rest, I have three sets of templates. One is for pure formatting; the .dotx templates in this group contain nothing but style decisions—what fonts and sizes and line spacing and margins to use for different elements—and they need to be attached to the file so as to override the equivalent items in the Normal template. When I start work on a job, I attach an edit-friendly style template to the files—one based on the client's own style template if there is one and using all the same style names, but formatting them for easy reading. That's the last I need to think about them if I'm using an edited version of the client's real template; checking the automatic-update box on the Templates and Add-Ins dialog will cause the formatting to snap back to the client's preferences when the file is opened there. If the template is one I made from scratch, at the end of the job I attach a template with the style names set to formatting that matches what the client wants to see, which keeps everyone happy.

I use macros for both operations, but it's quite easy to do manually—just click Attach in the top half of the Templates and Add-Ins dialog (in Document Template on the Developer tab, but still happily available at Alt+T, I) to get a list of available templates, and then double-click the template you want to use. Check "Automatically update document styles" on this dialog to make the text in your document take on the appearance specified for styles of the same names in the new template.

> *Note:* Word 2010 retains vestiges of the other automatic update feature, the one that takes local formatting changes like adding italics to a word and propagates them to every bit of text in that style, which will drive you mad. This feature is invisible most of the time, but the Word Happens imps sometimes put it on the Modify Style dialog to tempt you. In addition, it shows up fairly reliably on the New Style box, graciously offering you a chance to shoot yourself in the foot on your own creations. Figure 10 shows this, um, feature on the New Style dialog. If you see a check box labeled "Automatically update" near the bottom of any style definition dialog, *do not check it* unless you really want to see the effects of changes in formatting very, very rapidly every time you make them.

The second template set—basically, one file named My2010World.dotm and its backups—is for things I want the computer to handle the same way regardless of whether I'm on my own project or one for a client. This is where I

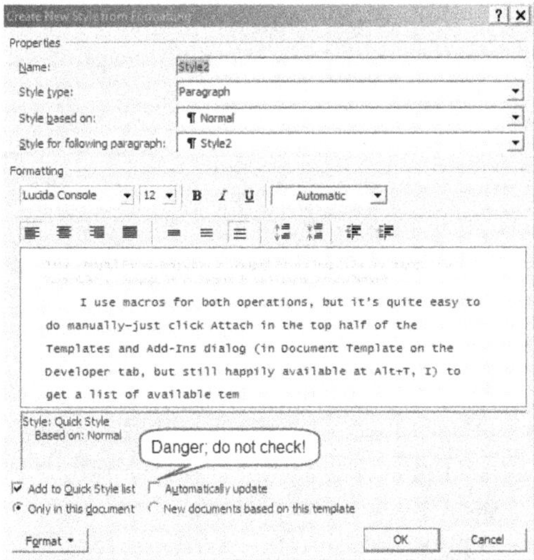

Figure 10. Auto-Update in a Style Dialog

keep all my utility macros—the ones presented in chapter 9 and others that do similar chores.

The third set is for macros designed so that I can click or type the same commands on every job but get different effects based on what each client wants. When I work on a manuscript, I use the bottom half of the Templates and Add-Ins dialog to load a *global template* (a template available to all Word files) designed for that specific client—called, unenterprisingly enough, "my[Client].dotm"—that handles a variety of standardizable chores. For example, these days everyone wants a copyeditor working on screen to do typemarking of some sort and put in queries to the author—but the formatting of the typemarking and the queries will differ dramatically from client to client. To take first-level heads, for example, my clients all want some combination of these approaches:

- Standard Word style "Heading 1" or client-specific Word style with a different name or "Normal" (which is as close as Word gets to no style at all)
- Typemarking code of @H1: or [H1] or <1> or <A> or no code at all
- Followed at the beginning of the next paragraph by @TX: or [TX L] or <GT> or no code at all (and perhaps also an unindented style or nothing else)

- And followed in the second paragraph by yet another code and a tab or a different style that includes an indentation decision—or not.

I don't want to use brainpower to keep track of that sort of thing, so every myClient template includes a macro that does whatever that client wants for a first-level head, and every myClient template has that macro assigned to Alt+1. When I perceive the need to typemark something as a first-level head, I press Alt+1, and Word provides whatever permutations of codes and styles that client has requested, then moves the cursor to the beginning of the first line of paragraph text—after the typemarking code, if any.

For queries I take the same approach—every myClient template has a macro called Queries that presents a dialog box with a range of choices, and the first choice in every Queries macro is a query to the author. The macro starts out with "1" already in the reply box, so pressing Enter after activating the macro gets me the most common choice with no further effort. The second choice is a query to the production editor, and then the list starts to vary by special things different clients tell me they need. Chapter 9 includes a macro that puts up a list of choices—no substantive content; it just has your computer ask you how you're feeling today—but it's easily modified to do whatever you need. And if you download the archive with the template files for this book, you'll get working choice macros for chapter openers, running text, and queries.

Global template gotcha: If you want to make changes to your selection of active global templates (that is, check and uncheck items listed in the lower part of the Templates and Add-Ins dialog box), the active document (if there is one) must be attached to a template on your system. Unlike earlier versions, Word 2010 will let you use the Templates and Add-Ins dialog with no file open, but when you try it with a file attached to a template that you don't actually have on your computer, it will go on strike. If you get a message saying the document template does not exist, press Esc to get away. Then you can switch to a document attached to one of your templates (Normal, for instance), or close the document, or save it as a template of the same name as the one attached (recommended when you want to create a variant set of styling and have the client's styling reappear when the file returns to its home computer).

Template Tussles

So Word uses templates to define styles and formats and all sorts of stuff.... How does it tell what template to consult at any given point? When you just stick with Normal.dotm, it's simple—that's the only template in play, and everything comes from there. But the system I'm recommending always has at least three templates active at the same time. Here's how they fight it out in Word 2010, which is different from what I knew (or thought I knew) of Word 2003 and earlier versions, and is no longer a pure hierarchy:

1. The template attached to the file (via Templates and Add-Ins, Attach—the top half of the dialog box) governs anything it addresses.
2. Normal.dotm comes in and operates the keyboard. Any hot keys you assign to macros or other features in Normal.dotm will override settings in other templates. (And boy was I surprised when one of this book's draft reviewers ran into that!) It still plays cleanup when it comes to style definitions and other things that Word needs to know and that aren't specified in the attached or global templates.
3. Then the current global templates (the ones you've instructed Word to list in the bottom half of the Templates and Add-Ins dialog box by clicking Add there, and then checked off to indicate you want them right now) do their thing with the keyboard. If two of them try to use the same hot key, Word sits there and sneers at you when you press the key—so make sure you keep your keyboard settings distinct for any non-Normal templates you might want to use at the same time. And don't put keyboard shortcuts in Normal unless you really really want them all the time, 'cuz that's what you're going to get.

Startup Templates

Anything you know you want to have at your fingertips (but not on the ribbon or QAT) every time you start Word should be in the Startup directory rather than in the one where you keep Normal.dotm and your client templates. I have to concede that I never made effective use of Startup in Word 2010 until this book was well under way, because it's tucked out of sight and keeping the contents up to date felt like too much hassle.

However, once I had an incentive to use it (see "Getting More without Asking" in chapter 9), it was easy. For Windows 7, use Word's File, Open dialog to navigate to C:\Users\[your username]\AppData\Roaming\Microsoft\Word\Startup and make it a Favorite so it will show up on the left pane of the dialog. For Windows XP, use Word's File, Open dialog to navigate to C:\Documents and Settings\[your username]\Application Data\Microsoft\Word\Startup, right-click in the Look-in pane, and click Add Startup. (If you've never installed a tool that calls for it, you may not have a Startup directory at all. In that case, simply create a directory with that name at the indicated location and proceed as described here.)

As soon as Startup was as quick to get to as the regular templates directory, I moved "My2010World.dotm" over there, making one less chore to do every time I open Word 2010. It saves more than a single box-check, too, as I usually didn't realize I'd forgotten to load it until I tried to use something in it—only to find that Word had downed tools and gone on strike.

Guided Practice with Templates

This section will get you started on a template collection, moving templates out of the "I don'wanna think about that" category for all time. If you've jumped straight here without working through the macro exercises, please turn to the macro "Setup" section and go through the steps listed there. In addition, please get the archive at http://www.powersedit.com/ftp/Word2010exercises.zip if you haven't already done so—anyone adept enough with templates to follow these exercises without using the files they're based on doesn't need these exercises at all! Unzip the archive and put the templates (the .dotm and .dotx files) wherever your computer keeps such things (discussed in "Using Templates" earlier in this chapter).

The Templative Style

As I've said, Word uses templates all the time whether you know it or not, so you might as well go along for the ride—they're what make the difference between a computer and a typewriter hardwired to a TV set. Use these steps to begin to get acquainted with them:

1. *Play with a style template.*
    a. Reopen WordWork.docx or whatever you were using for a garbage file in the macro practice.
    b. Press Alt+T, I to open the Templates and Add-Ins dialog.
    c. Click on Attach in the upper right corner of the dialog.
    d. Double-click on BasicCourier.dotx in the list of templates that opens.
    e. Check the Automatically Update Document Styles box when the system returns to the dialog.
    f. Close the dialog and observe the change in the file (which should suddenly look like it came off a typewriter).

g. Move the cursor to the beginning of the line that says "First-Level Head." Press Ctrl+Shift+[Down Arrow] to select the entire paragraph (all the text, plus the pilcrow at the end).

h. Press Ctrl+Shift+S to activate the floating Apply Styles box.

i. Start typing the name of the Heading 1 style in the box. As soon as "Heading 1" appears (probably right after "h"), press Enter.

j. Move the cursor to the line that says "Second-Level Head"; anywhere in the line will do. Do not make a selection.

k. Return to the floating box and press [Down Arrow] to get to "Heading 2" and then press Enter. (Note how you set the style for the whole paragraph whether you select it or not—meaning you don't really need to select it at all.)

2. *Scroll back up* to the third paragraph—the one that starts (and continues) "Long quoted passage…." Apply the Extract style.

3. *Make a new style template.*

a. Press Ctrl+F12, then click Templates on the left panel.

b. Open BasicCourier.dotx.

c. Press F12 and save as BasicLucida.dotx.

d. Press Ctrl+Shift+S to open the Apply Styles dialog.

e. Make sure Normal is showing in the Style Name box. (If it isn't, click the down-arrow beside the box, then find it in the list that opens.)

f. Click Modify to open the Modify Style dialog, and set the "New documents based on this template" radio button.

g. Click Format, then Font.

h. Change the Font Name to Lucida Console. To find the name, just start typing it in the box; as usual with this sort of dialog, the list of choices will jump toward what you're entering. Select the name when you see it.

i. Click OK twice, then click Close on the Apply Styles dialog.

j. Update the commentary on the text page to indicate the name of the font in use and note that you made the template from one of mine.

k. Close BasicLucida.dotx, allowing Word to save it.

l. Press Alt+T, I to reopen the Templates and Add-Ins dialog and attach the new template to WordWork.docx, making sure the "Automatically update document styles" box is still checked; observe the change in the file.

Templates for Action

Long ago, I read an otherwise unmemorable science fiction story that proposed a spiffy piece of tech: pilots design their own control panels, with all the virtual knobs and blinkenlights where they want them, and a standard control interface takes the input and output from the virtual panel and feeds it back and forth between the pilot and whatever vehicle is in use at the moment. Me, I'm not dead certain I'd want to trust my life to that level of automediation, but it works just fine in Word with global macro templates. (*Note:* This exercise is still looking for WordWork.docx—so if you took a break, make sure it's open before you get started.)

1. *Establish a global template.*

   a. Press Alt+T, I to reopen the Templates and Add-Ins dialog and click Add (middle right side of the box).

   b. Double-click ClientBase.dotm in the list that opens.

   c. Note that ClientBase.dotm now appears on the global templates and add-ins list, with a check mark beside it. Close the dialog.

2. *Play with the features built into the template.*

   a. Place the cursor on "First-Level Head" and press Ctrl+Shift+N to restore it to Normal style. Press Alt+1. Observe the change in the text and in the assigned style—visible on the QAT if you've put the style name box there as recommended earlier, or in the Style area pane if you're in Draft or Outline view and have used File, Options, Advanced, Display to open it up.

   b. Move to the end of the next paragraph, press Ctrl+Alt+comma, and type a few words—which will appear as tracked additions.

c. Press Ctrl+Alt+Shift+[comma] and type another word while the tracking is hidden, then press Ctrl+Alt+[comma] again.

d. Select one of the new words and press Alt+[period]; select another and press Alt+[comma]. Presto—you've just accepted and rejected revisions without going near the Review ribbon.

e. Place the cursor on "Long quoted passage" and press Ctrl+Shift+N to restore it to Normal style. Press Alt+Z, 2 and Enter to watch it indent itself. Then press Alt+Z and Enter and see what happens. (This template just uses Normal style for regular text.)

f. Place the cursor after any period and press Alt+Q and Enter. Note how you're all set up to start typing a query to the author.

g. Move up to the beginning of the WordWork file and copy "Scintillating Title" to the Clipboard—but not the pilcrow at the end of the line. Place the cursor at the top of the file and press Alt+Shift+P and Enter. Look ma, running heads!

h. Play with the other choices offered when you press Alt+Z, Alt+Shift+P, and Alt+Q.

3. *Turn the global template off and on again.*

   a. Press Alt+T, I and uncheck the box beside ClientBase.dotm.

   b. Close the dialog.

   c. Press Alt+Q. Watch Word sit and sneer at you. (That is, observe that the hot-key assignments reside in the template, which must be loaded as global for you to have access to them.)

   d. Press Alt+T, I and check the ClientBase.dotm box again.

4. *Make a second global template based on the first.*

   a. Press Ctrl+F12 and open ClientBase.dotm.

   b. Press F12 and save as My[clientname].dotm—where "clientname" is whichever client you plan to tailor your Word environment for first.

   c. Record one macro for an operation that client needs all the time—perhaps codes for a first-level heading and the following paragraph. If you do a heading, remember to change the style to Word's Heading 1, too—just make sure the cursor is in the heading line, then press Ctrl+Shift+S to open the Apply Styles dialog and start typing the style name until "Heading 1" appears on the line, then press Enter. (Call the macro "x" and let it default to Normal.dotm.)

d. Try the macro to see if it works. (See "Set Up a QAT Button for Testing Macros" in the "Macronipulation" section of this chapter if you've skipped the macro exercises and want a quick way to run macros you're working on.)

e. Press Alt+F11 to open the VBA editor. Double-click NewMacros in Normal if it isn't already open, and clean up your new "x" macro, changing or deleting lines of code that don't do what you want. (The recorder will pick up everything you do, including mistakes and unnecessary steps. If you're not sure if a line is needed or not, just type a single quote at the beginning to comment it out, and see what the macro does without it; that way, it'll be easy to restore if the macro stops working.)

f. When your macro is working properly, copy or cut it out of Normal. dotm. Double-click NewMacros in the My[clientname] VBA project and paste it in there. If it's taking over the job of one of the macros already there—say, H1—paste it over the old version. The simplest way to do this is to move the cursor to the beginning of the line following "Sub H1()," select the rest of the macro, and paste in your new version. Then delete the "Sub X()" line and you're in business. The change will work immediately, whether or not you save the template, but you will need to save if you want to keep the change beyond the current session.

g. Return to Word and press Alt+T, I. Add the new template to the global list at the bottom of the Templates and Add-Ins dialog.

h. As time allows, return to My[clientname].dotm and build in other things you need to do more than once or twice on each project for that specific client. If the client has told you to use its own style names, refer to them in the macros instead of to the Word built-ins. (Note that you will need to attach a style template with those names to the files for that client, as well.)

Template Tips and Tricks

As with macros, knowing how to use, change, and create templates is basically enough to go on with. Nonetheless, some background info will come in handy.

Updating Style Templates

Every feature of a style template is up for grabs. Play with styling the varying levels of heads, types of lists, and whatnot to see what they do. The exercise in the "Templates for Action" section just changes the base font, but that's barely the beginning.

Each new style defaults to being based on Normal, or on another style that was based on Normal, and it's easiest to leave things that way—whatever changes you make earlier in a chain cascade all the way through it. You can increase your control by designing a new default text style from scratch—based on "(no style)"—and basing things on that. Developing your own default will keep a client's Normal style from overriding yours—which isn't something copyeditors care about much, but it can be a factor for those producing print versions of documents. You can get even more control—at the price of even more work—by defining every style de novo, based on "(no style)," so that nothing cascades. Me, I let 'em base themselves on Normal.

Attaching Style Templates with Macros

I record macros that attach each of my style templates, and make sure that the one I use for most of my work has a name that sorts to the very top of the list (so Alt+F8, Enter always runs that macro and no other). The macro attaches the template, turns on revision tracking, and sets the zoom factor where I like it. (These days, I keep the template-attachment macros with the rest of my utility-macro collection in My2010World.dotm in the Startup directory—that way I can get at them without opening the corresponding myClient template first.)

Juggling Client Templates

When you start a new client template, copy the one most similar to the new requirements—that'll minimize the new coding.

Do not hesitate to add to each template; the book coding and chapter-opener macros are especially useful to stuff with all the options that might come up. For example, ClientBase.dotm has only three choices in the chapter-opener macro—but the client template I use most often has twenty-two. It looks horribly complex at first glance, but any given project uses only a few options, which are easy to store in short-term memory.

For the WordWork.docx file, try creating a chapter-opener macro that goes past the subtitle and codes the author, epigraph, and epigraph source lines. You might also prefer to have the macro change the Word style assigned to each line rather than (or in addition to) applying @-codes. It's all yours now....

6 Domesticating Tracked Changes

Of everything Word offers an aspiring editor, Track Changes probably evokes the most angst. It makes the screen look funny. It interferes with other aspects of using Word. It either imitates an accident in a paint factory or makes it almost impossible to tell who did what. It rats you out if you work at noon or midnight instead of standard office hours. What's an editor to do?

Suck it up.

With some minor care and adjustment of the settings, Track Changes is great stuff. You can reduce the look-funny factor a lot by the way you make each change; you can turn it off when it's going to make something else sick; you can (alas) get used to its peculiar color choices—or refresh them when they're too awful; you can ignore or hocus the time stamps. (I've never had any client mention them, but if one did, I'd just say, "Yes, I work odd hours. That's the advantage of being a freelancer." If push comes to shove, you can change the clock so the time stamps show what the client wants to see … but I'd have serious reservations about the value of a client who needed that sort of babying.)

Settings

The main thing to remember about your Track Changes setup is that it's yours—no choice of appearance you make on Review, Track Changes, Change Tracking Options will have any effect whatsoever on any other machine.

Unlike pre-2007 versions, Word 2010 does give you one item on the Track Changes Options dialog that alters the file itself, as opposed to what it looks like on your screen. If you remove the check mark from "Track formatting," Word reallyo, trulyo won't keep track of the formatting, and subsequent formatting changes in the file won't show up in the tracking. Unfortunately, unlike the rest of the options, that setting is file-specific; you can't tell Word to get out of the format-tracking business for good and all. (You can stop it for your own new files by opening Normal.dotm and clearing the format tracking there, but that won't touch your clients' files.) I've dealt with the problem by recording a macro to clear the "Track formatting" check box and hanging it on the QAT, using the nice little icon that looks like a closed eye—for "Go to sleep, dammit!"

But for the rest of the settings, it's open season. Use balloons or not. (I vote for not.) Format the tracking so you feel most comfortable. (Or least uncomfortable.) But unless you're the only one who will make tracked changes to the files you work on, do not pick a specific color. It looks as though you ought to be able to pick one of those wonderful colors for your own stuff and let your authors pick theirs, but that ain't how it works. If you pick a color, every tracked change—yours, your author's, your production editor's cat's—will show up in that color. (On your machine. If you like it, do it; it makes no never mind to anyone else. I use the dark red on my travel computer, where I'm almost always editing rather than dealing with author reviews, and where I'm often in lighting conditions that make Word's default color choice hard on the eyes.)

The only way to have Word clearly differentiate one reviewer from another is to set the colors for insertions and deletions to "By author"—the boxes on Track Changes Options that show up as half red and half blue. That does the job, but it turns you over to the Surprise Party Department in the process.

Here's how it works: Every time you start Word, that's a new session, and in each session, the author of the first change Word encounters is assigned the color red. That's why your own work is almost always red, and you might be tempted to go for something gentler, say, green.... The next author discovered to have changed anything anywhere almost always gets blue. After that, it's unpredictable for another seven colors, some of which—the goose-turd yellow and electric magenta in particular—are downright nasty, while others, like the regular green and the dark red, are quite pleasant. And if you should be so fortunate as to have a tenth reviewer in play during a session, just to put the cherry on top, number ten gets red again.

If the colors start to double up or a high-volume contributor to a file gets a color you hate to look at, just close Word and reopen it, and then open some other file (not the one you started with in the previous session) first. That will get you a new array of color assignments, quite possibly one that's easier to live with, and you'll be OK as long as all ten-plus reviewers aren't messing with the same file.... Alternatively, you can pick a color (knowing that it will apply to everyone) and mouse over any change whose source you want to know; if you have checked "Show document tooltips on hover" on File, Options, Display, under "Page display options," a little box will appear indicating who made the change and when.

Besides the color controls, you can use the Change Tracking options (at Review, Track Changes, down-arrow) to control the on-screen appearance of insertions, deletions, and formatting changes (if you're tracking the latter), and also the location of the "change bars"—the vertical lines in the margin that indicate whether anything in the corresponding lines of text has been changed. I like boldface insertions, strikeover deletions, no flag for formatting, and change bars in the left margin, but you can set these values to whatever you find congenial, secure in the knowledge that no one else will see what you have decided to do.

Word 2010 retains the default (introduced in Word 2002+) that makes the tracking visible in every file you open or save. I recommend keeping this, as it's serious CYA; it was introduced at the behest of law firms burned by releasing files with tracking and comments that should never have gotten out the door. If it really gives you hives, you can turn it off by going to File, Options, Trust Center, Trust Center Settings, Privacy Options and unchecking "Make hidden markup visible when opening or saving." You can get a similar effect by putting the commands that hide or display tracking on hot keys, however, and I recommend that alternative; it makes getting rid of the unwanted view into a quick key press, and you're never taken by surprise by what's in the file.

Keeping the Screen Sane

A comfortable author is a happy author, and a happy author makes for a happy editor. The appearance of your tracked changes can boost or lower your author's happiness level in a big way, so it's worth taking a bit of extra care to keep the screen as simple, uncluttered, and easy to read as you can. Figure 11 illustrates the techniques you can use to do this, and the following sections discuss them in more detail.

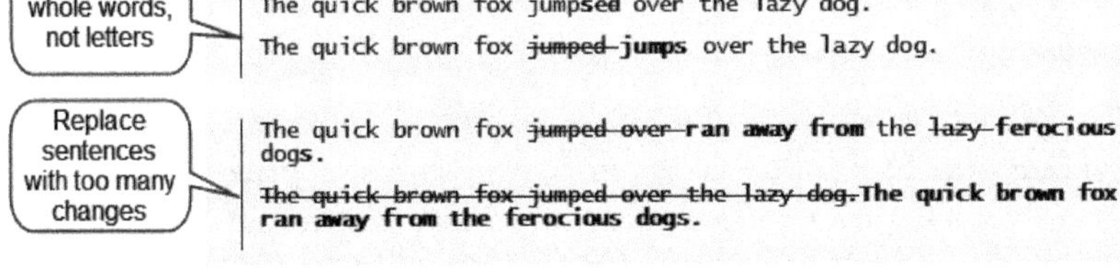

Figure 11. Taming the Tracking

When Nobody Cares, Nobody Cares

Publishers tend to require lots of corrections that don't change the semantic content of a manuscript. Things like the number of spaces between sentences, the spacing between paragraphs, the punctuation of quotes, and a raft of other mechanical things need to be set quite precisely for the page-makeup program, but they're not something the author should be concerned about.

So what you want to do is take them right out of play. If your client agrees, make all such changes with the tracking turned off, so the author isn't presented with page after page of change bars flagging things that need no attention. It's useful to skim the files at the beginning of a job to get an idea of the extent of this sort of thing, and to pick up on the more egregious typewriter relics: use of the spacebar instead of the table function or the tab key to line up tables, for example. That way you can plan your attack and take care of as much as possible up front.

Ideally, you want to turn the tracking on once and leave it on. If you keep it running but invisible, which often makes the edit much more congenial, it's amazingly easy to flip it off to deal with one little thing and then realize half an hour later that it's still off. (A point I'm reminded of forcibly all too often; shortly after I wrote the "Restoring Lost Tracking" section in this chapter, I had to apply its last-ditch advice on a live job.)

Make It Logical

When you're working on paper, it's logical up to a point to change the smallest error—for example, delete the "ed" at the end of a verb that ought to be in the present tense and replace it with "s"—but eventually it's better to just cross out the whole word and replace it. Likewise for a sentence with several words changed, and very occasionally even for a paragraph that's been well and truly carved up.

It's the same on the screen, but the point comes much sooner—replacing the entire logical unit (especially a word) is almost always easier on the author, and it needn't make noticeably more work for the editor. Two tricks make all the difference:

On File, Options, Advanced, Editing options, check "Typing replaces selected text": Then build the habit of selecting letters you want to replace in a word rather than backspacing over them or deleting them. It takes no more effort; the extra key press (Shift+arrow to select, as opposed to Backspace or Delete alone) is more than balanced by the layout of the keyboard—the Shift and arrow keys are easier to get to than Backspace or Delete. And when you select part of a word to change instead of erasing the letters, you get a whole new word, not just the letters you type, and that is much easier to read.

Record a simple macro to replace a selection with itself. This is one of the easiest to build and most useful tools you can have, and all it takes is selecting any text, then turning on the macro recorder and pressing Ctrl+X (cut) followed by Ctrl+V (paste). Turn off the recorder and give the macro a hot key—I use Ctrl+R for Replace—and use it whenever a sentence or part of a sentence gets hard to read because too many words have changed. You can also use it at the paragraph level—but sparingly, and just where you want the author to think about the whole statement as opposed to its parts. (For more on macros, read the "Macros" section of chapter 5.)

Remember Case

Word offers a handy-dandy command called ChangeCase that acts as a three-way toggle, changing words or selected text from lowercase to initial caps to all caps and back around to lowercase. It defaults to Shift+F3, but it's so useful that I keep it on Ctrl+[slash] so it's right under my hand. However, it has one, ah, feature that makes it either even more useful or too dangerous to use, depending on what you're working on: Track Changes cannot see it.

So if the author has misused case in ways that are utterly uncontroversial and not subject to question, you can use ChangeCase to normalize the text without crudding up the manuscript with a bunch of extra tracking. But. If the author's use of case might matter, keep your fingers off this shortcut. At least on the first appearance of a term that may need reevaluation, make the edit by selecting the initial letter and typing over it in the other case. That will show the old version of the word as wholly deleted and the new one as wholly added, making it much harder to miss. Then put in a query explaining the change to the author and asking if it's acceptable—and promising to fix it if it's not. (Whether to make subsequent changes blind—without tracking them—or not is a judgment call. You have to weigh the amount of work you save up front against the amount of hassle to find all the little devils later if it turns out you have to restore them.)

Abandoning the Review Tab and Reviewing Pane

The Review tab and Reviewing pane (like the equivalent dialogs in earlier versions of Word) are part and parcel of Word's oh-you-poor-dear-let-me-take-care-of-you approach to its users. On the ribbon, you can indeed do everything you might need to do with regard to tracked changes: move from revision to revision, accept and reject changes, adjust the kinds of things you see on the screen. But it's slow and cumbersome, inviting you to mouse around instead of keeping your hands on the keyboard. And the pane takes up a whole lot of screen real estate to show you what's already visible in the document; I've never figured out a use for it that makes it worth the space.

In Word 2010, I've just added the one item I find most useful—Display for Review—to the QAT, to give me a quick reminder as to the state of the tracking display. With the more limited toolbar space, I don't bother with the other items I used to keep on view in earlier versions of Word; it's so rarely necessary to use Show Markup to control which reviewers' work and what kinds of changes appear on the screen that I go ahead and use the Review tab for that, and the Accept and Reject icons are right there next to Show Markup if I need them. For the rest, moving from change to change during an edit review is easy enough by eye with the movement keys, augmented by Find, because you never want to stop at each and every change—just the ones you need to do something about individually. And I never use Word Comments, so I don't need those buttons at all. I use hot keys for most of the functions of the Review tab:

- *Turn Track Changes off and on*: Ctrl+Shift+E (a built-in hot key)
- *Turn off the display of tracking while keeping Track Changes running (or turning it on)*: Ctrl+Shift+Alt+[comma] (my own hot key; runs a recorded macro)
- *Turn on the display of tracking while keeping Track Changes running (or turning it on)*: Ctrl+Alt+[comma] (my own hot key; runs a recorded macro)
- *Approve a selected change*: Alt+[period] (my own hot key; runs a recorded macro)
- *Reject a selected change*: Alt+[comma] (my own hot key; runs a recorded macro)
- *Approve all changes remaining in a file*: Ctrl+A, Alt+[period] (a built-in hot key to select the whole file, followed by my own hot key to run a recorded approve-selected-change macro)

Note: I used to make a lot of use of the Accept Change button to clear changes in formatting, but I finally got a clear-tracked-format macro working—see "Clearing Tracked Format Changes" in chapter 9. The macro is rarely needed in Word 2010 since you can make it stop tracking formatting changes, but it can come in handy if you forget to turn off the tracking or inherit a file with a lot of tracked format changes along with tracking you have to keep.

Moving Text without Losing the Tracking

Sometimes you get a paragraph or so properly edited, only to realize that it really belongs somewhere else in the manuscript. Then you discover that if you cut and paste, you lose all the details; the original shows up as deleted, and the new location just has the edit.

To keep the tracking, all you have to do is turn off Track Changes (in both files, if you're moving something from one file to another). Cut and paste, and all the tracking will come along. Of course, the paragraph will look as though the text was always in the new spot and never in the old one, so it's a good idea to add tracked notes to the author at both points, explaining what got moved and where.

Word 2010 has a new feature that allows it to track moves, showing the old and new location in a different color from other edits, but it works only on blocks of text that are at least one sentence long and have no tracked changes. If the text has been edited before you move it and you leave the tracking on, you get the old passage showing as a simple deletion and the new one as an addition—with the edits themselves not flagged.

Restoring Lost Tracking

Murphy rules. If you occasionally allow yourself to stop the tracking "just for a moment," you will eventually forget to turn it back on again at the end of the moment. What you do next depends on how much work you did before you spotted the goof.

If it's just a paragraph or so, you're probably best off pressing Ctrl+Z (Undo) repeatedly until you get back to the last edit that you tracked, then turning on the tracking and repeating the work. If your memory is like mine or if you've done enough work to overload your memory, that will be more of a chore than you're likely to want to deal with from scratch; in that case, before you start undoing things, make a copy of the edit you forgot to track and paste it into a new document so you can use it as a guide for the replacement.

For a longer lapse, your only friend is Compare—and it ain't that much of a friend. It looks like a good idea:

1. Save the edited file, then Save As a copy and approve all changes in it, and save and close the copy.
2. Make a new copy of the untouched original, clear any tracking that the author may have left in it, and rerun any changes you deliberately made without tracking them—spacing and format changes and whatnot. (If

you find you need to do this often, make a habit of keeping an interim set of files that include only the untracked changes to the originals.)

3. Go to Compare on the Reviewing ribbon and follow the prompts, identifying your edit copy as the Compare target.

If you have lived a truly virtuous life, the active document, now bearing the name of the edit copy, will appear on your screen with all the changes tracked in the right direction (things removed from the original showing as deleted, and new stuff showing as added). Once you confirm that this version of the file is usable, you can save it and then rename it so it's the primary edit file.

Alternatively, you can manually copy the changes into the file you were working on when you noticed the lapse. Why would you do this manually? Unfortunately, Compare has always been a fragile and fractious beast. I don't have direct experience of it in Word 2010, but I would be surprised to find much improvement. When it gets lost, it starts designating huge swatches of text as added or deleted, losing all the internal detail. That's doubly true if one editor or reviewer has edited another person's edits. And you won't catch all the blind changes, no matter how hard you try: if nothing else, Compare is sensitive to the ChangeCase alterations that Track Changes doesn't spot.

If the reconstituted copy is too awful to use, you have one more chance:

1. Make a copy of the untracked part of the edit and paste it into a new file.
2. Make a copy of the corresponding part of the original—using the one you prepared for the first Compare effort—and paste it into yet another new file.
3. Run the comparison again, working from the partial copy of the original to the partial copy of the edit. With less input, Compare has a better chance of working properly.
4. If you get a usable passage, make sure Track Changes is turned off in the marked-up file and the full edit file, then copy and paste the text over the edit you forgot to track. Don't forget to turn Track Changes on again!

And if it's still too full of garbage to show the author, all you can do is decide whether it's worse to redo the work or apologize for losing the tracking….

Protecting Tracked Changes

So you put your twenty or forty or eighty hours into making the very best edit you can … and then you send the files back to the author. That's gotta be scary. (At least as scary as it was for the author to send it off for editing, but that's another story.) What if the author just gets rid of everything you did? Or even some of it?

Some publishers still avoid this issue by sending authors only a printout of the edited files. The author marks up the hard copy by hand—providing any extensive changes on disk if the editor responsible for processing the author's review is very, very fortunate—and someone sits down when it comes back and types, scans, or otherwise inputs all the changes.

But if the author does get the files back—and more and more do—it's useful to do something to try to make sure the edit doesn't just disappear, either accidentally or deliberately. Once again, Word is there to help.

What Word does is allow you to "protect the file for tracked changes," which prevents anyone from turning off the Track Changes facility. I use the macros given in the "Protecting for Tracked Changes" section of chapter 9 for this, but you can do it directly on a file via "Restrict Editing" in the Protect group of the Review tab. In the task pane that opens on the right side of the screen, check the box under "2. Editing restrictions," then select "Tracked changes" in the drop-down list that becomes accessible. When you click the "Yes, Start Enforcing Protection" box under "3. Start enforcement," Word will open a dialog box for setting a password. (You can skip the password if you prefer, but in that case anyone can just turn the protection off again.) Protection for tracked changes also disables the approval and rejection buttons in the Changes group of the Review tab.

With the file protected for tracked changes, the author can still add or delete text, but only out in the open. If you decide to go this route, the main worry is forgetting or mistyping the password; the macros in chapter 9 will allow you to automate the process, so you never get it wrong.

> *Note:* Word 2010 lacks the loophole described in *Making Word Work for You*, the earlier version of this book, so it's no longer possible to use macros to approve and reject changes in a protected file.

Publisher clients generally request protection, so the authors have no beef with you, and you can persuade most private clients that the protection helps them make sure they don't inadvertently lose their investment in the edit. (Which is true; it's the author's book, and an author who's buying an edit can insist on any text at all—there's no need to sneak.)

Removing Tracking from an Edited File

The big strength of Track Changes is the way it eliminates the need to retype accepted edits in the final version of the file. Once you address all the points the author raises about an edit, adjusting or removing revisions as needed and erasing any queries you've put into the file, you can approve everything else holus-bolus and go your way rejoicing.

Well, almost. It's unfortunately easy to screw up the spacing around tracked changes, leaving too many or too few spaces or lines around places where changes were tracked in the file. Many of the resulting problems will surface in a final run of the spelling checker, so you should always do that *after* clearing the tracking. But—yet more unfortunately—the spelling checker won't catch everything. To get at the things it misses, I run some wildcard searches on each file, looking at each hit to see if it's OK or not. (They can't be cleared globally, because some of the things each one finds will be correct already, and the ones that aren't may need different corrective actions at different points in the file.) I use the first two of the four "Find what" strings in the following list with material that uses Word styles for coding, and the last three if the material is using @-codes ("@H1:" for heading one, for example):

```
.[! ^013^0146^01480-9\)<\[\]]
([!.:\?0-9\!^0146^0148\)\]])^013
[!0-9^013•]^t
^013[!^t\@•]
```

You may need to tweak these strings to fit the requirements of your own clients. The first string finds periods that are not followed by a space, hard return, single or double closing curly quote mark, number, closing paren, open angle bracket, or square bracket. The second finds hard returns not preceded by a period, colon, question mark, number, exclamation point, single or double closing curly quote mark, closing paren, or closing square bracket. The third finds tabs not preceded by numbers, hard returns, or bullets, and the fourth finds hard returns that are not followed by tabs, @ signs (used to delimit typemarking codes by some clients), or bullet characters. For more help deciphering these strings, see the boxed list of special characters in the "Find and Replace" section of chapter 3.

If you try this approach, type in everything in the strings precisely, including the square brackets, and remember to select the "Use wildcards" check box in the Find and Replace dialog. Rather than looking up these horrible strings and typing them in every time, I spare my memory and fingers by putting them in as AutoCorrect blocks, with the triggers !2 and !3, respectively—for "not these two" and "not those three." To use a set, I type the trigger at the beginning of the first manuscript file and let AutoCorrect put them onto the page, then cut and paste the resulting output lines one by one into the "Find what" line of a wildcard search. After I've searched that file for each one, making whatever adjustments it needs, I close the file and repeat the searches one after another on the other files, taking advantage of the down-arrow beside the "Find what" line to restore earlier search strings.

7 Coping with Snares and Pitfalls

For an editor, Word comes close to Churchill's definition of democracy: the worst system available, except for all the others. It has towering strengths—but great weaknesses and problems as well. Here's the cream of the crud—and what to do about it.

Simple Insanity

Word 2010 still sometimes goes bonkers. That is, some or all of the commands suddenly stop getting the effects you've learned to love (or at least expect) and instead do other things entirely. What have you done wrong?

Nothing.

What caused the fit? In the computer's working memory and in the file itself lurk forty-two gazillion electronic whatsits, each required to be in a specific state, and any of which can make a program or an individual file "behave unpredictably" (computer-speak for "get all screwed up") if it gets out of whack. So when things do behave unpredictably, chances are that somewhere in its little insides, your computer has lost its place, and messages and commands meant for one bit of software are reaching another.

When unintended results appear, waste no time figuring out exactly what's wrong—anything you see is almost certainly just a symptom of a generic problem with a generic fix that falls somewhere on this list:

1. *Press Esc.* Often, the Escape key is all it takes to restore Word to a sense of its duty. If that doesn't work…
2. *Close Word and reopen it.* Open the file you were working on. If it's back to normal, you're home and dry.
3. *If it's not, open another file.* If *it's* normal, skip to step 5. If both files are screwed up, close Word and rename your Normal.dotm file; any name will do, as long as you can recognize it and not confuse it with one of your deliberate backups. Reopen Word, letting it generate a new, all-default Normal.dotm. If Word is still misbehaving, go on to step 4. If Word is OK with a default Normal.dotm and you have a customized backup of Normal.dotm from before the problem started,

close Word again, delete or rename the newly generated Normal.dotm you'll find in the template directory, make a copy of your last good backup (not the one you just renamed), name the copy "Normal. dotm," then restart Word and go your way rejoicing.

4. *Close Word and the rest of the programs you have open, then restart your computer and open Word again.* Check both misbehaving files. If they're both OK now, you're back in business, except that if you had a customized Normal.dotm file, you'll probably want to close Word one more time, delete Normal.dotm, and restart with a renamed copy of the last good Normal.dotm backup. If the "warm boot" didn't fix things, shut everything down, including your operating system, turn off your computer, and wait sixty seconds. Turn it on and try again (a "cold boot"). If the second file you opened is not back to normal, go to step 9. If it's OK but the original file is still screwed up, go to step 5.
5. *See if inserting the file leaves the garbage behind.* Open a new blank file, with the tracking turned off. Make sure the tracking is also turned off in the problem file, close it, and press Alt+I, L to activate the old Insert, File dialog and put a copy into the new file. Save it under a new name, close it, and reopen it; if it's back to normal, save it under the working name and you're done. If not, go on to step 6. (On the ribbon, you can find this function on the Insert tab: in the Text group, click the down-arrow next to Object, and choose "Text from File.")
6. *Save the file in rich text format (.rtf), close it, and reopen it.* If it seems OK, save it as .docx and see if it's still corruption-free when you close and open it again. If not, go on to step 7.
7. *Try "Open and Repair" to find out if Word can scratch its own itch.* That is, go to File, Open, and use the down-arrow beside the Open button to get to the "Open and Repair" option and see if the Word fairies can help you. If not, you're in do-it-yourself territory with step 8.
8. *"Maggie" the misbehaving file.* That is, turn on the display of hidden text so you can see the paragraph marks, then select and copy everything in the file except the very last paragraph mark. Open a new blank file and paste in what you just copied, then close the new file, saving it under a new name. Close the old file. Open the new one. If it's OK, you're clear, and you can save it under the working name. If it's not, repeat the procedure one section at a time, copying everything up to each section break except for the last paragraph mark

in a section. (Alternatively, you can copy everything before the last paragraph mark except the graphics, section breaks, and tables into a single new file, making a note at each point as to what you left out. This rules out whole classes of content that are likelier than the text to be corrupt.) If you've made a series of smaller files and any of them are still misbehaving, repeat the procedure on those files one paragraph at a time (or divide them in half if they have lots of paragraphs, and keep subdividing until you've isolated the problem). The divide-in-half procedure also works on whole files that have no section breaks, or too many to make them useful divisions. If so much is misbehaving that there seems no end to the trouble, go to step 9.

Alternatively, if you're working with a .doc file and you really don't want to ask for help (or you've a yen for more of the history of a file than its author probably wants you to see), go to File, Open, select the file name, and set the file type box to "Recover Text from Any File." That will lose all the formatting in the file but will at least extract the text—and at the end, you'll see all the metadata the file has accumulated, including who saved it and on what version of Word. To keep the results of this maneuver, you need to save the file deliberately (under the old name or a new one); Word doesn't offer to save the file for you if you just close it.

> *Note:* The trick doesn't work with .docx files. It produces an endless list of character strings with almost no semantic content, apparently because it hits the compression the .docx format uses under the hood and barfs.

9. *Yell for help.* Specify the version of Word you're using and the operating system, and be as clear as you can about what seems to be wrong and what you've done about it. If framing that message doesn't make you smack your forehead and fix the error yourself, and your usual sources of help run dry, try one of the sources listed in chapter 8.

I tend to apply the process in this order because—given the number of programs I keep open all the time—I really hate to shut down the computer. But the whole thing is worth trying before making the slightest effort to see if you might have done something wrong yourself—that is, something that makes Word produce the peculiar results you see by obeying your instructions—which is the kind of thing you're apt to find out when you call for help.

And if all else fails and you are looking at ripping out the program and reinstalling it, there's one last option. I haven't tried it myself, but the Microsoft Knowledge Base article "How to Reset User Options and Registry Settings in Word" (http://support.microsoft.com/kb/822005) may help you walk your copy of Word back to the land of peace and productivity.

Personal Exposure

Word 2010 still figures that you're proud of who you are and what you've done, and you want others to see it. Most of the time, it's correct; you're happy—or at least not unhappy—with the results. But sometimes you'd really rather hide. And sometimes your ID gets split, so it looks like there were two or three of you on the job, adding to the tangle of colors displayed when Track Changes is set to "by author," and it'd be a kindness to pull yourself together.

If all you want to do is hide your identity, Word 2010 makes it reasonably straightforward—assuming you also want to remove the built-in record of the date and time you were working and the template attached to the document. For some documents, you can just go to File, Options, Trust Center, Trust Center Settings, Privacy Options and check "Remove personal information from file properties on save." If that line is grayed out, go to File, Info, Check for Issues, Inspect Document, Inspect; that will get you to a screen that will let you anonymize the file.

However, if what you want is to resorb the evil twins left by working with the file on different computers, you need to work on the naked guts of a text file. Save the file in rich text format (*.rtf) and open it in your text editor. (I use the freebie Notetab Light, available at http://www.notetab.com, for the purpose. However, as Shmuel Gerber—one of my reviewers—points out, you could use Word to do the text editing of the .rtf file; just go to File, Options, Advanced, General and check "Confirm file format conversion on open," and then choose "Plain Text" format when opening the file.) Search for the string

*\revtbl

and skip over the word "Unknown." Change the variants on your name in the list that follows to the one you want to show up, and then save the modified .rtf file. When you open it in Word, you'll be whole—and you can save the file back to .docx and get back to work. And if you just want to change your name to "Your Friendly Copyeditor" or somesuch and leave the rest of the properties intact, the revtbl-edit trick will let you do it.

If you were so incautious as to leave Comments as you worked on different computers, you'll need to find each one you want to change in the .rtf command string. Change the name after \atnauthor (and the initials after \atnid if they're also a problem).

> *Note:* It pays to subscribe to discussion lists, despite the impact on your online inbox. I never in a million years would have figured out this technique on my own, but Shmuel Gerber posted it to Copyediting-L (http://www.copyediting-l.info/) in mid-2011, and I knew it'd come in handy one day. He cited *Word Hacks: Tips & Tools for Taming Your Text*, an O'Reilly book by Andrew Savikas, and while drafting this paragraph I ordered a copy for myself, kicking myself for not thinking of that earlier. It proved an interesting read, but it focuses on Word 2003 and thus wasn't as useful as I hoped.

Protected View

Word 2010 has a new, ah, feature designed to keep you safe whether you want to be that safe or not. Every once in a while, you'll get a message to the effect that your document has opened in Protected View, meaning that it's essentially uneditable. I find it hard to keep the details of digging out from this problem in my head, so I consult Microsoft when I need a refresher. See http://office.microsoft.com/en-us/word-help/what-is-protected-view-HA010355931.aspx (http://tinyurl.com/MSProtects).

Automatic Numbering

Automated lists in Word sort of work, but they're finicky and temperamental, and every discussion I've read agrees they've been broken from the get-go and are broken still.

When they work, the automated lists are enormously helpful, so authors like them a lot. Much better than trying to remember to keep the numbers straight by hand—particularly while you're adding, deleting, and shuffling list items! And if a list is the only one in a file, it probably won't misbehave.

Unfortunately, multiple lists tend to get on each other's nerves, sometimes to the point of making Word refuse to restart the numbering when told to do so or otherwise lose track of how the lists should look. When that happens, it's not anything you did wrong, and there's no one way out of the hole; just fiddle with the file until you get something you can use. In a pinch, you can switch from the regular automatic numbers to field codes, which work much more reliably. You can find instructions in "Word 2007: Using SEQ Fields for Numbering" at http://cybertext.wordpress.com/2010/03/08/word-2007-setting-up-seq-fields-for-numbering-pt-1/ (http://tinyurl.com/SEQfields). Despite the reference to Word 2007 in the title, the article also addresses Word 2010.

People who really need numbering to work—law firms and the like—tend to buy an after-market product to take care of it for them. Most publishers want the numbers converted to regular text during the edit, so editors can get along with a simpler tool. "Freezing Automated Lists" in chapter 9 includes a very basic conversion macro, and the Editorium (discussed in chapter 8) has a more elaborate tool called "ListFixer" that I've often seen recommended, though I stick with my own version.

Fields at Play

As noted, one way authors get around the problem with automated lists is to use field codes: snippets that translate to different values of text depending on internal or external conditions, and that are good for lots of things in addition to lists. Field codes are not broken; they work quite nicely—but not for publishers, as they invariably make the page-makeup stage of production cough up its guts. So all a publisher's editor needs to know about fields is how to recognize them and how to get rid of them.

Hyperlinks behave like fields in many ways (and you can kill them along with the rest of the fields), but they're not quite the same beast. The main pitfall they offer is their persistence; several apparently logical countermeasures just conceal them without actually cutting them. I heard of one document where the author had put in a dummy—but active—hyperlink full of x's to indicate that it was a fake. The text was later deleted, but the spot in the file stayed live … and curious readers clicking the little hand that mysteriously appeared there were taken straight to a porn site.

Recognizing Fields

These two steps will put fields under your hand:

In File, Options, Advanced, Show document content, set "Field shading" to "Always." That will turn the background of the screen a different color behind a field, so you can tell what you're dealing with.

Place the "View Field Codes" command (from the All Commands list) on the QAT. That will let you toggle all the fields in the document between their calculated values and their formulas at one click, which can be very useful if your author has employed EndNote or some other add-in that uses fields to accomplish something in the files. You can get the same effect by pressing Alt+F9, but I prefer to keep it on the QAT as I don't use it enough to get the key combo to stick in my mind.

You don't need to do anything about hyperlinks to make them visible; they show up as blue underlined text if you haven't changed the default.

Killing Fields

To remove one field at a time: Select the field and press Ctrl+Shift+F9.

To remove all the fields from a file at one stroke: Press Ctrl+A to select all the text, then press Ctrl+Shift+F9. Alternatively, you can pick up the "FreezeField" macro from chapter 9 and use that instead. (This won't touch the headers and footers, where page numbers are generally set in fields. You can usually ignore fields in headers and footers, as those parts of the file don't affect page makeup. Unfortunately, this method won't touch embedded endnotes either; to get rid of fields there, you need to select the embedded notes as a group separately and use either the command or the macro.)

To remove a hyperlink and replace it with its text: Move the cursor into the linked text, then press Ctrl+K to get to the Insert Hyperlink dialog and Alt+R to break the link.

To make sure you don't inadvertently insert new links: Press Alt+T, A to open the AutoCorrect Options dialog, click the AutoFormat As You Type tab, and make sure the box for replacing Internet and network paths with hyperlinks is not checked.

Weird Little Squares

Sometimes you'll open a file only to see a sprinkling of blank squares in the running text. The squares indicate that the author has put in characters that aren't in the font you're using, which is good to know—but not nearly enough to go on with.

Before you call for help, try copying a square to the Clipboard and pasting it onto the "Find what" line of the Replace dialog; Word will often show you what the square represents and allow you to replace it with a similar character you can read. You can also select the square, go to the Insert ribbon tab and click the down-arrow at Symbol, and then click More Symbols at the bottom of the list that appears. If Word can interpret the character, it will show up on a dialog box that includes the name and character code of the symbol. If those ploys fail, pasting the unknown into a search engine may get you an explanation.

Replacement is often a good idea—squares may just be hiding weird bullet characters or punctuation marks that didn't survive the transition from one word processing system to another, so switching to a readable equivalent will have no effect on the meaning. If you discover that you're dealing with a letter from another alphabet, however, it'd probably be a good idea to check with your production editor (if you're fortunate enough to have one) or your author to discuss the best way of dealing with it.

Undead Text

So you're editing along, Track Changes active but out of sight, and you select and type over an ill-chosen word. Unbeknownst to you, the formerly adjacent word, already deleted and now hidden in the tracking, reappears on the screen behind where you're working, just as though you'd typed it in again on purpose. You, of course, looking where you're going and not where you've been, see nothing, and later wonder how you could have been such a doofus.

This eerie resurrection of text happened a lot in Word 97. It was rarer in Word 2003 and is rarer still in Word 2010 … but I'm sure I've seen it fairly recently. The word *you're* seems to have an especially strong grip on the afterlife. Not a whole lot you can do about this; it's a real-for-real crawling bug. Just be aware of the possibility, and if you think you see it, it's not you that's buggy.

Char Char Char

As far as I can tell, Word 2010 no longer creates the garbage "char" styles generated by Word 2002 and 2003—but you may still run across them, so it's worth knowing what happened. The old versions generated brand new character styles when you selected part of a paragraph and assigned a paragraph style (instead of the character style you should have used) to your selection. That is, Word decided that you wanted to create a whole new character style with the same font attributes as the paragraph style, and named it "[paragraphstylename] Char" to make the connection clear. Do it again, and you'd get "[paragraphstylename] Char Char"—and so on.

This caused all sorts of problems. The crud on the styles list was bad enough, but it was also a threat to the underlying style. If you deleted the char version, Word happily deleted the original paragraph style, too. The character and paragraph styles were linked; changes to one automatically propagated to the other.

Word 2003 hid the char styles but still created them, essentially putting a comforting piece of black tape over the problem indicator. Word 2010, praise be, will let you delete a char style (when you find one in an inherited document) without pulling the string and deleting the real style it's based on.

8 Locating Useful Additions

With so much available within Word, you need more? Yup. Not need, perhaps—but there's a lot out there that will make your editing even faster and more congenial than it is with everything introduced thus far.

Your Computer as Indentured Servant

I'm not the only one to have spent years devising ways to make my computer pick up the grunt work of editing so I could concentrate on the interesting bits. And some of these experts have put in the extra hours needed to program and document their insights well enough to turn them into products worth a working editor's consideration.

Editorium

Most of my experience is with the Editorium (http://www.editorium.com). Jack Lyon's Editor's Toolkit Plus product is probably the equivalent of three years' intensive experience and experimentation with customizing your system to make it fly—plus several tools that are beyond most do-it-yourself macro programmers.

If you're just starting out and your copy of Word 2010 is pretty much plain vanilla, give Editor's Toolkit Plus a try—free for forty-five days, then less than a hundred bucks to keep; a week of playing with it should put you ahead of a class that costs several times as much and runs half a year. And take a look at the Freebies section of the site, too.

It was a grief to me that I had about five years' intensive customization in my system when I first discovered the Editorium, so it felt like too much mental retreading to rearrange my reflexes to yet another new keyboard. (I've since learned that the Toolkit customizations include many of the function keys, so its users need to be prepared to find new homes for some of the displaced tasks.) What I've done instead is pick up several of his stand-alone tools:

FileCleaner: Offers an array of choices for getting rid of typewriter-brained errors in edit files—including bad spacing and lowercase "l" instead of numeral "1"—that (like all of Jack's stuff) you can apply to a single file, a set of open files, or all the files in a directory.

MegaReplacer: Takes your list of find-and-replace decisions (regarding text, character formatting, or styles) and applies it to the usual array of files. You can choose whether or not to track the results, and whether to let the routine run by itself or stop and ask you about each decision. You can also save the list for future use—or delete it once you're done with it. This is the product I use for the first step in chapter 1 as a way to wipe out global errors in a manuscript.

→ 1.a

MultiMacro: Applies your list of macros in the order you specify. The protection-for-tracked-changes macros in chapter 9 rely on this add-in for effortless and complete application to a whole book's worth of files.

NoteStripper: Converts footnotes and endnotes from Word's embedded facility to plain text—and vice versa, so they renumber themselves. Pays for itself the first time an author decides to delete note 3 and note 68 of 175 and scatter a few new notes through the chapter at the last minute.

Puller: Gives you a list of delimited items—things in parentheses, straight or angle brackets, or other codes you specify—which is especially useful for checking up on your typemarking. You can see every single one you used, identified by file, or get a consolidated list stripped of duplicates.

RazzmaTag: Converts Word formatting to user codes and vice versa. It's designed for tagging files for QuarkXPress and other typesetting programs, so I make little use of it; but it's handy when it's handy—if only for its ability to generate a bunch of files in plain text instead of Word format.

WordCounter: Gives you a table of word, character, and both Word-generated page counts and counts calculated based on 250-word pages for the usual array of files; essential for figuring project rates. (It will also give you a concordance of a file, with or without the number of times each word was used.)

These are all tools, not wizards, so they take some practice to use effectively. But they all come with detailed manuals and help screens—and if you run into trouble, you can always write to Jack and get an answer (or a fix, if you've found a new problem).

> *Note:* If you're an old Editorium fan just converting to Word 2010, use the installation routines built into the packages you're transferring. Don't get clever and load the templates in the place you think they should go (the way I did); Word 2010 will ignore them unless you get them planted properly.

Intelligent Editing

I've worked a bit with Daniel Heuman's PerfectIt (http://www.intelligentediting.com), a Windows-only tool that does a lovely job of flagging internal inconsistency in a document so you can choose which version you prefer. For example, it picks up inconsistent hyphenation (say, short-term or short term), as well as a variety of other issues such as capitalization in headings and single words, abbreviation definitions, and bullet punctuation. It can also generate a table of abbreviations automatically from your text.

It would have saved my tail on my career's one disastrous editing failure—a book on dinosaur sex and reproduction that I loved working on, but that was so full of small differences in the middle of multi-syllable names that I lost track of everything else—and there was a lot else. With PerfectIt to catch the transpositions in the middle of fifteen-letter words for me, I'da been way ahead.

Unfortunately (or fortunately, or as a result of careful screening), most of my work since the release of PerfectIt hasn't involved that sort of complexity. The program also works best with all the chapters of a manuscript in one file, and most of my work has been in separate chapter files. But take a look at the product—the thirty-day free trial could solve that problem you're having right now, or give you an extra burst of confidence that you've caught everything you meant to catch....

WordsnSync

Rich Adin of WordsnSync (http://wordsnsync.com/)put his kids through college as a freelance editor, and he has built a truly amazing array of tools for vetting specialized spelling, checking journal titles (in just about any style you can think of—Chicago, AMA, APA, PubMed), and taking care of a host of other chores efficiently enough to make scholarly editing into a viable business. I haven't worked with them—the niche I've built rarely involves that sort of demand, and the tools I already had when it came out were working too well for me to overcome my mental inertia.

Were I starting out with on-screen editing, or currently editing without the aid of tools, or tempted by a project requiring the kind of precision Rich's EditTools 5.1 brings within easy reach, I would certainly give it a try, patting myself on the back for maintaining a Windows system (the only environment where it'll run). The fifteen-day free test drive would be enough for a good taste of the macros. The add-in databases (for drugs, organisms, and journals) must be purchased—so I'd start the test drive without them, then pay for them if it looked likely that I'd get the underlying package. Asked to comment, Rich pointed out that although the main element of the package, encouragingly called "Never Spell Word," comes configured for medical editing with tabs labeled for organisms and drugs, users can rename them to focus on other sorts of editing.

The whole thing would cost less than a hundred bucks. Alternatively, the Editor's Toolkit Ultimate package would cost about a hundred-fifty and include licenses for Jack Lyon's Editor's Toolkit Plus and Daniel Heuman's PerfectIt, too.

Paul Beverley

Paul Beverley started out in about my league—facing more editing chores to do than time he wanted to spend on them—so he began to write macros to help him along. However, being more energetic and public-spirited than I, he took them to a point where others could use them, published them, and then refined them and added features—several times—as freebies for the working editor. I've rarely used them myself, being well supplied with tools and somewhat embarrassingly set in my ways in my semi-retired state, but they come highly recommended. Daniel Heuman's site has a great write-up on the collection—see http://www.intelligentediting.com/editfasterwithmacros.aspx. You can pick up Paul's (currently) 600-page book at http://www.archivepub.co.uk/macros.html. For a glimpse of his work, see "Converting Any Integer to Text" in chapter 9.

Other Support Programs

Word add-ins aren't the only game in town. A working editor should have a variety of software besides Word to help get the job done. Books could be (and have been) written about every one of the issues I list here; this is the merest sketch of the kinds of things to think about.

Basic Security

It's a bad old world out there. When your livelihood depends on your computer, protect it—against viruses, spyware, and other invaders. At the moment, I'm still a bit surprised to say, I'm using the free Microsoft Security Essentials as my sole firewall and antivirus software. It came with my new travel laptop and worked nicely there, and the tech who upgraded my main system to Windows 7 said it still had a good rep. I continue to stay away from Internet Explorer as much as possible (and Outlook entirely; I use Firefox and Thunderbird instead) and to use an ISP (Earthlink) that's pretty good at keeping the do-bads at bay. I also subscribe to Brian Livingston's Windows Secrets newsletter (http://windowssecrets.com)to stay current with Microsoft's adventures, though I don't always follow his advice.

File Transfer

These days, most jobs involve e-mailing files back and forth, but for very large files or relatively slow connections, you'll probably find e-mail inconvenient. At that point you'll want a file transfer protocol (FTP) manager, which will allow you to hook up to a website directly and download or upload your files. Before upgrading to Windows 7, I used FTP Explorer from http://www.ftpx.com, an inexpensive and easy-to-use program that allows drag-and-drop file transfers, downloading in the background, and other useful features—but haven't yet gotten around to looking for it in Windows 7, as my browser has been up to my needs. I also subscribe to Dropbox (http://www.dropbox.com/home)which provides a convenient location to leave and acquire files.

Backup

Computers get more and more reliable every year, but there's still truth in this sad maxim:

A hard drive that has never crashed is a hard drive that hasn't crashed yet.

And even short of a drive crash, any number of things can come between you and the files that earn you your living. I use Carbonite (http://www.carbonite.com/en/v2/index)for running backups, and copy crucial files to a portable hard disk as well whenever they're updated.

Optical Character Recognition

A scanner is such a good toy, it's pleasant that it's business-related. The more often you receive work on paper, of course, the more useful a scanner is; but eventually almost any editor will find it handy to be able to suck words off paper without using the eye-hand input process. Most scanners come with some sort of optical character recognition (OCR) software, but it's a good idea to take a look at the top-of-the-line paid version of the freebie. Notwithstanding that advice, I have to admit that I'm still using the program ABBYY FineReader Lite (http://www.abbyy.com)that came with my new scanner.

Dictionary

If you're working in a specialized field, you may be able to buy a dictionary add-in that will augment Word's spelling checker with the terminology of the field. Ask on one of the editors' mailing lists, and your remote colleagues will advise. In addition, regular dictionaries (such as *Merriam-Webster's Collegiate Dictionary, 11th edition*) now come with CDs that you can run instead of reaching for the book to look something up, or you can purchase downloads or online access instead; that seems to be the wave of the future. I still use the paper version, however—because it makes a good break to call on my big arm muscles—instead of the finger-twiddling screen-lookup variety.

Reveal Codes

CrossEyes from Levit & James opens a panel very similar to WordPerfect's Reveal Codes pane—but goes WP one better, as it will hide all the text except that adjacent to changes in formatting. I was reluctant even to try this product for years, as I'd found ways to live without Reveal Codes and figured the best CrossEyes could do would be a translation, subject to error of its own. But a demonstration was impressive, and if I had to deal with the details of formatting, I think I'd find it worthwhile. Especially since it's free now.

You can read more about it and download a copy of CrossEyes 5 at http://www.levitjames.com/Products/CrossEyes.aspx. The Levit & James site only mentioned working with Word 2007 when I looked, but I asked and was assured that the product works with the 32-bit version of Word 2010. If you're using the 64-bit version, you're out of luck; it doesn't work with that—illustrating the dangers of living on the cutting edge. (I'm a trailing-edge techie myself.) For more info, see the manual, available at http://www.levitjames.com/WebServices/download.asmx/DownloadFile/69667201-6ddc-48b7-8d9c-7349d64982ca/readme50.pdf (http://tinyurl.com/CrossEyesPDF).

Compression Managers

If double-clicking a compressed file's name doesn't make it open, Windows users should download a program to deal with .zip files. I use WinZip (http://www.winzip.com), which isn't free but does have a trial period. Something along these lines is an indispensable part of modern computing.

Another excellent compression manager is 7-Zip, a free, open-source program by Igor Pavlov. It supports its own native .7z format as well as a multitude of other formats, including .zip. You can download the latest version from http://www.7-zip.org.

For background on what zip utilities do and why you need one, see http://office.microsoft.com/en-us/infopath-help/zip-or-unzip-a-file-HA001127690.aspx?CTT=1 (http://tinyurl.com/WhyZip).

Books and Resources

Word 2010 is a living exemplar of my father's favorite maxim:

**It's supposed to be easy.
If it's not easy, you're doing it wrong.**

He was referring to tools and mechanical things, but it holds true for software. Whatever you have to do in Word should be nearly effortless—and if you don't know how to make it effortless, you need more information. And even if it already seems pretty much effortless, you still can use more information—much of what I know about Word's byways comes from a habit of subscribing to any source of free and reasonably reliable info that crosses my path. Here are some places to turn when just asking Word 2010, via the sometimes-useful Help system, doesn't get you what you need:

Jack Lyon, *Macro Cookbook for Microsoft Word.* Softcover book that walks you through the basics of making, using, and scavenging macros in more detail than I've had room for here—a good next step in your quest for Word domination. It's available at the Editorium site, http://www.editorium.com. (You can subscribe to his newsletter and search the newsletter archives there, too.)

Geoff Hart, *Effective Onscreen Editing: New Tools for an Old Profession, 2nd ed.* The big book on on-screen editing—the PDF runs more than seven hundred pages. It's full of general advice on the business of editing, plus information on how to use any word processor to make your life easier, with specific techniques illustrated using Word as an example. To order, visit Geoff's website (http://www.geoff-hart.com). While you're at the site, have a look at Geoff's Resources page (http://www.geoff-hart.com/resources.html)—lots of useful info there, including the full text of many of his articles on technical writing, editing, information design, backup and security, and even avoiding repetitive stress injuries, all linked from the bibliography section at the top of the page.

Allen Wyatt, *WordTips.* Free e-mail newsletter from http://wordribbon.tips.net/, which also has a link to other tips and net offerings, including a number of inexpensive and useful collections of hints and tools.

Word-PC. Free e-mail discussion group for users of Word on PC equipment—good for heavy-duty advice and macro programming tips. To join, send a blank e-mail message to word-pc-subscribe-request@liverpool.ac.uk; "blank" means no text, no sig line, nothing.

Shauna Kelly was another online Word wiz who helped a lot of people over the years. Although she died in 2011, her site (aptly called "Making the Most of Word in Your Business") is still up as a memorial, and it provides clear and cogent answers to common questions—starting with a page that offers so many entry points that it works even if you're not sure of the question: http://shaunakelly.com/word/index.html. It also still has links to use to ask her a question directly, which seems a little eerie. (Questions posed via these links don't get answered, so ignore them.)

Other Web Resources

Microsoft's "Word Macros and Visual Basic for Applications FAQ" (http://word.mvps.org/FAQs/MacrosVBA/index.htm)addresses lots of the questions that may arise.

Microsoft's "Interactive: Word 2003 to Word 2007 Command Reference Guide"—http://office.microsoft.com/en-us/word-help/interactive-word-2003-to-word-2007-command-reference-guide-HA010074432.aspx?pid=CH100487431033 (http://tinyurl.com/CommandXRef)—gives you a mock-up of the Word 2003 screen; clicking menu items and toolbar buttons gets you the location and name of the Word 2007 equivalent. Since the ribbon locations mostly stayed stable during the upgrade to 2010, the interactive guide is still useful despite being slightly out of date. (The site also includes a downloadable workbook with even more commands than the on-screen version presents.)

The Office Watch "Word 2010 Command Finder" (http://news.office-watch.com/commandlist/Word_2010.aspx) lists more than 1,700 commands along with where to find them if you're looking to bind them to a hot key—and what to use to invoke them if you're writing VBA.

9 A Bouquet of Sample Shortcuts

My first and most important shortcut set isn't here. It's a package of four macros—originally written for WordPerfect for DOS and later redone for WordPerfect for Windows and again for MS Word—that make it possible to consolidate a book's worth of chapter-level bibliographies in one file, sort them together, pull out the parts of references that identify edited collections so they can be dealt with as a separate group for consistency, restore them to their original reference entries, deal with all the various errors chapter authors have made in the references as a whole, and then restore all the references, in their proper order, to the chapters they came from. The set is too temperamental for general release, but it works—I've used it successfully on manuscripts whose chapters collectively carried upwards of a thousand reference items.

I mention it here only because it marks a defining moment in my on-screen editing career. On my very first commercial electronic edit, I spent twelve hours on the bibliographies for a journal whose time budget—the amount of time I could afford to spend and still make the lowest effective rate I felt good about—was twenty hours. (No, I didn't finish within my time budget on that one!) It was painfully clear that I faced a choice—either I had to tell the client I wouldn't do that sort of job again, or I had to find a better way.

On screen, there's always a better way. This chapter provides a collection to get you started. If your computer has ever run a Word 2010 macro, the easiest way to use these little jewels is to copy the text from "Sub" through "End Sub" and then press Alt+F11 and paste the text at the end of the NewMacros list. That won't work on a computer utterly innocent of macros, however; in that case, press Alt+F8; type the macro name; click Create; paste the text over the lines that say "Sub [macroname()]" and "End Sub" in the resulting screen; and close out the screen. (Note that any line that begins with a single straight quote mark is for you to read, so you can understand what the next lines do; your computer will ignore it.) For more detailed instructions, work through the exercises in chapter 5—which create what may be the all-time most useful copyediting tool: a pair of macros that let you put in a serial comma as soon as you see the need for it, without moving the cursor to the end of the word preceding the commaless "and" or "or." (In addition, the downloadable exercise archive for that chapter includes the text of each of the macros given here, so you won't need to type them in.)

Adding “ing”

In the course of smoothing out a sentence, it’s often useful to change a present-tense or past-tense verb into a gerund, but selecting the unneeded characters and typing in “ing” rapidly gets old. With this macro on a hot key, all you have to do is put the cursor where you want the “i” and turn it loose. You may have to fiddle with the punctuation if there’s a comma or period after your word, but that’s a small chore and rarely needed.

Sample 1: IngyDingy()

```
Sub IngyDingy()
' Macro recorded 10/22/2005 by Hilary Powers
    Selection.MoveRight Unit:=wdWord, Count:=1, Extend:=wdExtend
    Selection.TypeText text:="ing"
End Sub
```

Checking Citations

As promised in the example in chapter 1, the first of the following macros allows you to select a whole citation or group of citations with one hot key—after you put the cursor at the beginning, which may be inside or outside the parens with the date. The second picks up the selected text, copies it to the other open document, advances to a new line there, and then returns to the main document and moves just to the right of the next opening paren.

→ 1.b

Sample 2: Fillerup()

```
Sub Fillerup()
' Macro cannibalized by Hilary Powers 1/30/04
Selection.Extend
Selection.Extend Character:=")"
End Sub
```

Sample 3: GetThat()

```
Sub GetThat()
' Macro recorded 1/29/2004 by Hilary Powers; the Window-switching
' line (which won't record properly in Word 2003 or Word 2010)
' refixed per Jack Lyon of the Editorium, 1/30/2004
Selection.Copy
WordBasic.NextWindow
Selection.PasteAndFormat (wdPasteDefault)
Selection.TypeParagraph
WordBasic.NextWindow
Selection.MoveRight Unit:=wdCharacter, Count:=1
Selection.Find.ClearFormatting
With Selection.Find
```

```
.text = "("
.Forward = True
.Wrap = wdFindContinue
End With
Selection.Find.Execute
Selection.MoveRight Unit:=wdCharacter, Count:=1
End Sub
```

Doing Nothing

If you wind up with a built-in hot key that does something you're sure you don't want, you can take it out of play by assigning this macro to it. (Much safer than putting something you do want to do there, as that risks trouble if you're ever on someone else's system.)

Sample 4: DoNothing()

```
Sub DoNothing()
' I'm empty
End Sub
```

Maintaining a Style Sheet

One of the joys of electronic editing is the ease of preparing a style sheet, but the cut-and-paste sequence can still get tiresome after a while. In the following macros, the first copies selected text and places it on the style sheet (the second of the two documents you have open for this trick), then stops there so you can add the part of speech or otherwise adjust the pasted text. The second puts a blank line in the style sheet and moves to it, returns to the main document, and clears the selection.

Sample 5: StyleThat()

```
Sub StyleThat()
' Macro adapted from GetThat by Hilary Powers 1/30/04
Selection.Copy
WordBasic.NextWindow
Selection.PasteAndFormat (wdPasteDefault)
End Sub
```

Sample 6: HedOnBack()

```
Sub HedOnBack()
' Macro adapted from GetThat by Hilary Powers 1/30/04
Selection.TypeParagraph
WordBasic.NextWindow
Selection.MoveRight Unit:=wdCharacter, Count:=1
End Sub
```

Protecting for Tracked Changes

Here are the macros for setting and removing protection for tracked changes (as promised in chapter 6). You can run them on one file at a time, but they work best when combined with the Editorium's MultiMacro product. Paste your own choice in between the quotes where the macros say "mypassword," which I assure you is not what I use.

Sample 7: trackpassword()

```
Sub trackpassword()
' Macro recorded 05/05/03 by Hilary Powers
   ActiveDocument.TrackRevisions = Not ActiveDocument.TrackRevisions
   ActiveDocument.Protect Password:="mypassword", NoReset:=False,
Type:=wdAllowOnlyRevisions
End Sub
```

Sample 8: trackrempswd()

```
Sub trackrempswd()
' Macro written 05/05/03 by Hilary Powers
If ActiveDocument.ProtectionType = wdNoProtection Then GoTo Last
    ActiveDocument.Unprotect Password:="mypassword"
Last:
End Sub
```

Coding Running Heads

Although requirements for telling the pager or page-makeup program what to use as running heads—the lines at the top of each book page that give the book or chapter title, or some other constant information—tend to differ from publisher to publisher, it's simplest to have the coding macros in a central location instead of the client template so you can copy one to another. I used to keep them in Normal.dotm, where they're easiest to get at and edit, but now they're in my utility-macro template.

Here's one version (longer than it needs to be because it also demonstrates the use of commented-out instructions). To use it:

1. Copy the book title and paste it into the text of the macro, where the comment indicates. (You can then run the macro over and over for each file in the project; just remember to change the title for the next book.)
2. Open a chapter file and copy the main title to the Clipboard, but not any following punctuation or the hard return at the end of the line.
3. Place the cursor at the beginning of the first line of the file. (It's OK if there's text on the line, but the cursor needs to be before the first character or things will get strange.)

4. Run the macro, using whichever technique seems easiest. (I keep it as the first choice on the list generated by the chapter-opener macro described in chapter 5.)

Sample 9: Runhead()

```
Sub Runhead()
' Runhead Macro
' Macro recorded 02/21/99 by Hilary Powers
    Selection.TypeText text:="@RHR:"
    Selection.TypeParagraph
    Selection.TypeText text:="@RHL:"
   With Selection.Font
'  Note - following lines are commands that are commented out.
'      .SmallCaps = True
'      .Italic = True
   End With
    Selection.TypeText text:="Reinventing Your Board"
'      Plug in book title between quotes on preceding line.
    Selection.TypeParagraph
    Selection.MoveUp Unit:=wdLine, Count:=2
    Selection.EndKey Unit:=wdLine
    Selection.Paste
    Selection.HomeKey Unit:=wdLine
    Selection.MoveDown Unit:=wdLine, Count:=2
    ' Selection.TypeBackspace
End Sub
```

Ignoring Unwanted Formatting

The default Paste operation (Ctrl+V) carries over the formatting of the copied material. Often this doesn't matter as you're pasting stuff that already matches the format in the new area, or you want the original formatting on the copy. But when you don't, it's a royal pain to get rid of the imported formatting, which may even affect adjacent material in your file. I keep the following macro on Ctrl+0 (that's zero on the regular keyboard) and use it whenever the old formatting would be a nuisance.

Sample 10: UnformatPaste()

```
Sub UnformatPaste()
' UnformatPaste Macro
' Macro written 2/24/2004 by Hilary Powers
' Because Word wouldn't record it
    Selection.PasteAndFormat (wdFormatPlainText)
End Sub
```

Clearing Tracked Format Changes

Word 2002 and 2003 insist on tracking changes in formatting if you're tracking anything at all, which makes clearing the tracking after author review much more difficult. It's not so much of a problem in Word 2010, since you can make that version stop tracking, but if you wind up with tracked formatting you want to get rid of, the following macro will do the job.

Sample 11: AcceptFormatChanges()

```
Sub AcceptFormatChanges()
' Macro cobbled up 8/14/2006 by Hilary Powers
' Based on commands revealed by Keri Morgret
' Use only on file that opens with all markup visible!
' Next four lines toggle all display of changes off.
    WordBasic.ShowFormatting
    WordBasic.ShowInkAnnotations
    WordBasic.ShowInsertionsAndDeletions
    WordBasic.ShowComments
' Toggle display of formatting back on.
    WordBasic.ShowFormatting
' Approve formatting changes.
    WordBasic.AcceptAllChangesShown
' Next three lines toggle everything else back on.
    WordBasic.ShowInsertionsAndDeletions
    WordBasic.ShowComments
    WordBasic.ShowInkAnnotations
End Sub
```

Freezing Fields

Word fields (including hyperlinks) bounce when they hit page-makeup programs, so it's useful to know how to convert them to plain text. (Pressing Ctrl+Shift+F9 also works on a selected item, and you can press Ctrl+A first to a select a whole file so you can clear all the fields in it—but you can feed this macro to the Editorium's MultiMacro tool and fix a whole directory at once.)

Sample 12: FreezeField()

```
Sub FreezeField()
' Macro recorded 03/28/02 by Hilary Powers
Selection.WholeStory
Selection.Fields.Unlink
End Sub
```

Unlinking Hyperlinks

Sometimes you get a file with fields you want to keep along with hyperlinks you want to get rid of. Rather than chasing the links one by each, you can use this little jewel from anywhere in the open file; no need to select text first.

Sample 13: RemoveHyperlinks()

```
Sub RemoveHyperlinks()
' Macro provided by Katharine O'Moore-Klopf to Copyediting-L.
    Dim aStory As Range, iLink As Integer
    For Each aStory In ActiveDocument.StoryRanges
        For iLink = aStory.Hyperlinks.Count To 1 Step -1
            aStory.Hyperlinks(iLink).Delete
        Next
    Next
        End Sub
```

Freezing Automated Lists

Word makes it easy for authors to create bulleted and numbered lists, but the feature is fugitive; page-makeup programs can't use it. If your client insists on real bullets and numbers, this macro will give them to you. The first line after the comments will do the basic job, but while its numbers are OK as is, its bullets are in Symbol font, which can be a problem. I used to give just that first line and recommend recording Find and Replace steps to change the bullets into another font, but Word 2010 (like several of its predecessors) has lost the ability to record font information in a Find and Replace operation. You can use the lines that specify font names here as models for other macros, if you need to work with fonts via macros on your system.

Sample 14: FreezeList()

```
Sub FreezeList()
' First line is macro contributed to Grapevine by Iwan Thomas 9-8-2000
' Converts autonumbered paragraphs to normally numbered paragraphs,
' and autobulleted paragraphs to paragraphs with real bullets. Basic
' bullets are in Symbol font, and are corrected via additional steps
' recorded 10/06/00 by Hilary Powers using Word 97. Word 2010 will not
' record this code. Other bullets may need further correction to get
' them into an acceptable format.
    ActiveDocument.ConvertNumbersToText
    Selection.Find.ClearFormatting
    Selection.Find.Font.Name = "Symbol"
    Selection.Find.Replacement.ClearFormatting
    Selection.Find.Replacement.Font.Name = "Courier New"
    With Selection.Find
        .text = ""
        .Replacement.text = ""
```

```
        .Forward = True
        .Wrap = wdFindContinue
        .Format = True
        .MatchCase = False
        .MatchWholeWord = False
        .MatchWildcards = False
        .MatchSoundsLike = False
        .MatchAllWordForms = False
    End With
    Selection.Find.Execute Replace:=wdReplaceAll
    Selection.Find.ClearFormatting
    Selection.Find.Replacement.ClearFormatting
    With Selection.Find
        .text = ChrW(61623)
        .Replacement.text = "."
        .Forward = True
        .Wrap = wdFindContinue
        .Format = False
        .MatchCase = False
        .MatchWholeWord = False
        .MatchWildcards = False
        .MatchSoundsLike = False
        .MatchAllWordForms = False
    End With
    Selection.Find.Execute Replace:=wdReplaceAll
End Sub
```

Converting Selected Text to an Alternative

Sometimes you have text that needs to be changed in some instances but not in others, so a global Find and Replace won't work. At the touch of a hot key, this macro will take any specific thing and change it to any other thing you name. You can set up items to serve as toggles; note that toward the end of the macro, selecting "U.S." will trigger a change to "United States," while selecting "United States" will trigger a change to "U.S." It does only the one thing it finds on its list based on your selection, so there's no chance it'll go bonkers and start grinding out the toggle items over and over.

The original of this macro converted integers from 1 to 99 to words, but I no longer use it for that purpose as Paul's version (given next) is much better. I left in a couple of numbers to illustrate the difference in the Case name depending on the content of the string to be converted: Case names that convert items including any text or spaces need to be enclosed in double quotes.

This version is too stripped-down to be much use, but it's a valuable core. If you copy the text for "20th" and repeat it for the other ordinal numbers you're likely to deal with, and do the same for “20s” and other plurals, you’ll have something that will come in handy quite often.

Sample 15: Converter()

```
Sub Converter()
' Based on macro written by Hilary Powers, June 2000
Dim vTarget As String
If Selection.Type = wdSelectionIP Then
MsgBox "Select something to convert first."
GoTo Last
Else
vTarget = Selection.text
End If
Select Case vTarget
Case 1
Selection.TypeText text:="one"
Case "1st"
Selection.TypeText text:="first"
Case "20th"
Selection.TypeText text:="twentieth"
Case "20s"
Selection.TypeText text:="twenties"
Case 100
Selection.TypeText text:="a hundred"
Case "00 "
Selection.TypeText text:=" hundred "
Case "000 "
Selection.TypeText text:=" thousand "
Case ",000 "
Selection.TypeText text:=" thousand "
Case "U.S."
Selection.TypeText text:="United States"
Case "US"
Selection.TypeText text:="U.S."
Case "United States"
Selection.TypeText text:="U.S."
End Select
Last:
End Sub
```

Converting Any Integer to Text

This macro will give you the text equivalent of any number with six digits or less. It works if you trigger it from anywhere before the number, but it will stop when it gets to punctuation—so delete the comma if you want it to work on a four- to six-digit number.

Sample 16: NumberToTextbyPaul()

```
Sub NumberToTextbyPaul()
' By Paul Beverley
' Version 26.12.12
' Convert next number into text
oldFind = Selection.Find.text
oldReplace = Selection.Find.Replacement.text
' Find a number (six figures max)
Selection.End = Selection.Start
With Selection.Find
  .ClearFormatting
  .Replacement.ClearFormatting
  .text = "[0-9]{1,6}"
  .Forward = True
  .MatchWildcards = True
  .MatchWholeWord = False
  .MatchSoundsLike = False
  .MatchAllWordForms = False
  .Execute
End With
' Create a field containing the digits and a special format code
Selection.Fields.Add Range:=Selection.Range, _
   Type:=wdFieldEmpty, text:="= " + Selection + " \* CardText", _
   PreserveFormatting:=True
' Select the field and copy it
Selection.MoveStart Unit:=wdCharacter, Count:=-1
Selection.Copy
' Paste the text as unformatted, replacing the field
Selection.PasteSpecial Link:=False, DataType:=wdPasteText, _
   Placement:=wdInLine, DisplayAsIcon:=False
With Selection.Find
  .text = oldFind
  .Replacement.text = oldReplace
  .MatchWildcards = False
End With
End Sub
```

Getting More without Asking

As promised in chapter 3, here are the macros that force Word 2010 to give you the whole Find and Replace dialog instead of the stripped-down, don't-trouble-your-poor-head version. They need to be in a template in your Word Startup folder to work their magic. (See "Startup Templates" in chapter 5 for info on getting this set up.)

Sample 17: AutoExec()

```
Sub AutoExec()
' Written by Jay Freedman to help David Chinell
' solve the expanded Find and Replace dialog problem,
' January 2013
Application.OnTime When:=Now + TimeValue("00:00:02"),
Name:="EditReplaceMore"
End Sub
```

Sample 18: EditReplaceMore()

```
Sub EditReplaceMore()
' Written by David Chinell, January 2013
Application.ScreenUpdating = False
SendKeys "%M"
Dialogs(wdDialogEditReplace).Display TimeOut:=10
Application.ScreenUpdating = True
End Sub
```

Offering Specific Choices

Sometimes you want the computer to ask you what to do next. One way to get this effect is to write a macro that asks for your input, then does one thing or another depending on your reply. You can take the following example and expand it to any number of options, and replace the "Case" text with the guts of any macro (the text between—but not including—"Sub" and "End Sub") to do whatever chore you have in mind. Alternatively, the "Case" text can be limited to "Call [othermacroname]" as described in "To Run a Macro inside a Macro" in chapter 5. Remember to update the "strTitle" to pose your new question and edit the "strPrompt" lines so the user knows what to choose.

I get much more mileage out of this type of macro in Word 2010 than I did in earlier versions, as it takes the place of the user menus where I kept lists of things specific clients wanted done. Word 2010 stuffed my user menus onto the Add-Ins ribbon tab, which put them farther from my fingertips than seemed convenient.

Sample 19: ChoiceShell()

```
Sub ChoiceShell()
' Macro written by Hilary Powers 02-09-04. Updated 03-04-08 by David
' Chinell to add action for Cancel button and clean up the code.
Dim strTitle As String
Dim strPrompt As String
Dim strDefault As String
Dim strResponse As String
' Set the InputBox variables
strTitle = "How are you feeling?"
' The "+ vbCrLf" code says prompts continue on the next line.
strPrompt = "1. Fine" + vbCrLf
strPrompt = strPrompt & "2. Frustrated" + vbCrLf
strPrompt = strPrompt & "3. Sick"
strDefault = "1"
' Get the user's choice
Do While strResponse = ""
' Make sure next bit (strResponse thru strDefault) is on one line.
    strResponse = InputBox(Title:=strTitle, Prompt:=strPrompt,
Default:=strDefault)
    Select Case strResponse
        Case ""
            ' Exit as Cancel was clicked
            Exit Do
        Case "1"
            ' Do stuff for choice 1 here
            Selection.TypeText text:="Great! Let's get to work!"
            Selection.TypeParagraph
        Case "2"
            ' Do stuff for choice 2 here
            Selection.TypeText text:="Take a deep breath...."
            Selection.TypeParagraph
        Case "3"
            ' Do stuff for choice 3 here
            Selection.TypeText text:="Take two aspirin and call me "
            Selection.TypeText text:="in the morning."
            Selection.TypeParagraph
        Case Else
            " Invalid selection. Null out response and prompt again.
            strResponse = ""
    End Select
Loop
End Sub
```

10 Walking Through a Job

Every edit is different … but they tend to follow a pattern, with certain kinds of chores most useful at certain times. Here is a rough outline of what I'd expect to do on almost any manuscript:

1. *Set up the job.*
    a. Get the files—probably by e-mail, these days, or downloaded from the client's FTP site.
    b. Run your virus checker before opening anything—or even moving the files out of the download directory. (I suspect that modern virus checkers do this during the download process, but check-this-now is still an option, and I find it comforting.)
    c. Set up a directory for the project—with, at minimum, a subdirectory for the untouched original files. (I keep the working files in the main project directory, where they're easy to get at.)
    d. Look over the hard copy (if there is any; it's nice but not essential to have it), and transfer any notes from the client to the files.
    e. Start the style sheet. I keep a master sheet for each client with the essentials of that client's requirements already filled in, and make a copy of it for each job. (Figure 12: Sample Style Sheet Master shows an annotated sample, and there's a copy without the markup in the archive of files described at the beginning of chapter 5.)
2. *Do a preliminary cleanup.*
    a. Run a mechanical setup macro to work around the author's typewriter-use habits. (Jack Lyon's FileCleaner is good if the client doesn't specify a setup set.)
    b. Turn on Track Changes.
    c. Do generic fixes via MegaReplacer, telling it to track the results. (My global-replace file includes things like changing *advisor* to *adviser* and *email* to *e-mail*—so as to fix stuff authors almost universally do and publishers equally universally avoid. The tracking makes it

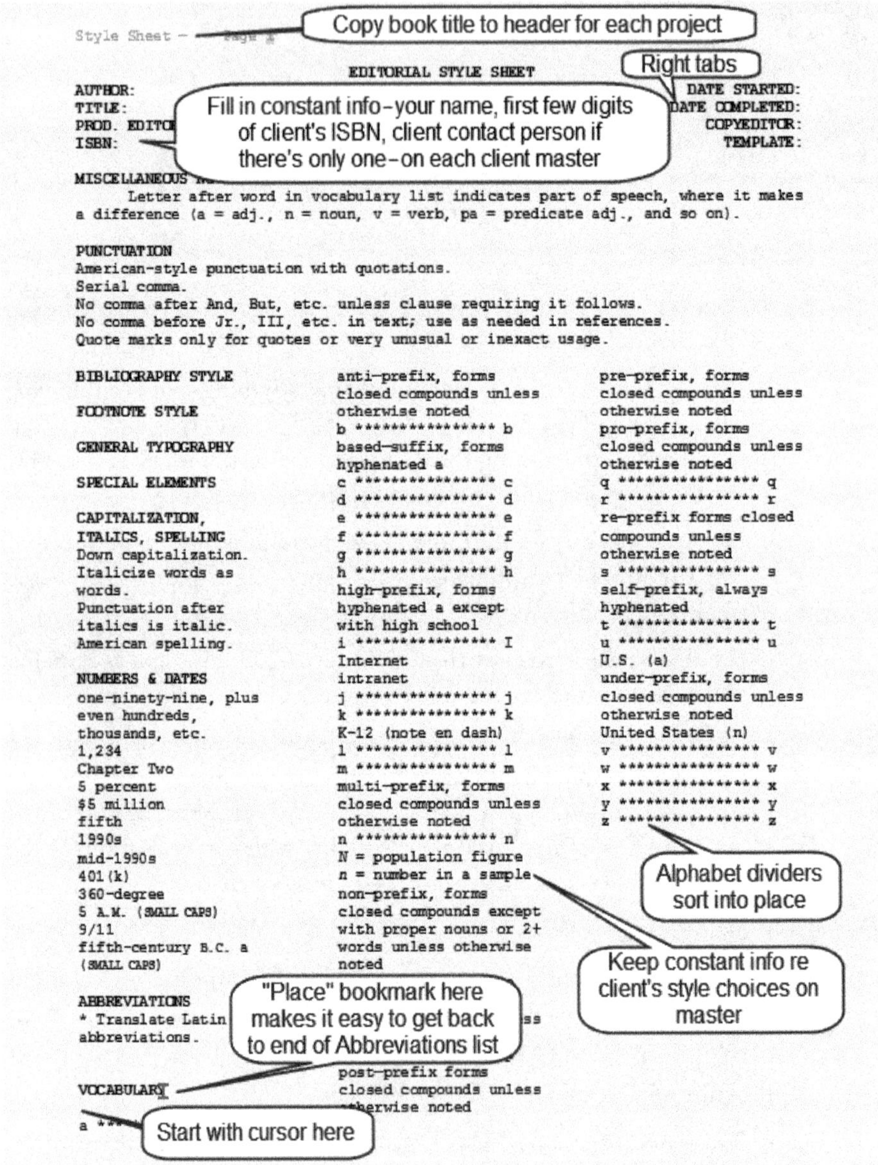

Style Sheet — Page 1

EDITORIAL STYLE SHEET

AUTHOR:
TITLE:
PROD. EDITOR
ISBN:

DATE STARTED:
DATE COMPLETED:
COPYEDITOR:
TEMPLATE:

MISCELLANEOUS
Letter after word in vocabulary list indicates part of speech, where it makes a difference (a = adj., n = noun, v = verb, pa = predicate adj., and so on).

PUNCTUATION
American-style punctuation with quotations.
Serial comma.
No comma after And, But, etc. unless clause requiring it follows.
No comma before Jr., III, etc. in text; use as needed in references.
Quote marks only for quotes or very unusual or inexact usage.

BIBLIOGRAPHY STYLE

FOOTNOTE STYLE

GENERAL TYPOGRAPHY

SPECIAL ELEMENTS

CAPITALIZATION, ITALICS, SPELLING
Down capitalization.
Italicize words as words.
Punctuation after italics is italic.
American spelling.

NUMBERS & DATES
one–ninety-nine, plus even hundreds, thousands, etc.
1,234
Chapter Two
5 percent
$5 million
fifth
1990s
mid-1990s
401(k)
360-degree
5 A.M. (SMALL CAPS)
9/11
fifth-century B.C. a (SMALL CAPS)

ABBREVIATIONS
* Translate Latin abbreviations.

VOCABULARY

a ****

anti-prefix, forms closed compounds unless otherwise noted
b **************** b
based-suffix, forms hyphenated a
c **************** c
d **************** d
e **************** e
f **************** f
g **************** g
h **************** h
high-prefix, forms hyphenated a except with high school
i **************** I
Internet
intranet
j **************** j
k **************** k
K-12 (note en dash)
l **************** l
m **************** m
multi-prefix, forms closed compounds unless otherwise noted
n **************** n
N = population figure
n = number in a sample
non-prefix, forms closed compounds except with proper nouns or 2+ words unless otherwise noted
...ss
post-prefix forms closed compounds unless otherwise noted

pre-prefix, forms closed compounds unless otherwise noted
pro-prefix, forms closed compounds unless otherwise noted
q **************** q
r **************** r
re-prefix forms closed compounds unless otherwise noted
s **************** s
self-prefix, always hyphenated
t **************** t
u **************** u
U.S. (a)
under-prefix, forms closed compounds unless otherwise noted
United States (n)
v **************** v
w **************** w
x **************** x
y **************** y
z **************** z

Figure 12. Sample Style Sheet Master

easy to undo any changes to titles and quotes, which need to stand as-was.)

d. Load or attach any client-specific or editing-environment templates.

3. *Edit the references so that each entry in the file follows the style laid down for the book.* (Doing this up front primes my brain with the vocabulary of the job and gives me a feel for how carefully the author has worked.)
4. *Consolidate the text citations, as described in chapter 1, step 2.* (To break up the effort, I usually do this chapter by chapter, before starting the first pass on the text of a chapter, not all at once.)
5. *Make the first edit pass.* (That is, read word by word and do whatever the assignment requires as you go.)

   a. Copy and paste terms reflecting decisions on usage, hyphenation, and whatnot to the style sheet. (Using macros like the ones in chapter 9.)

   b. Fix characteristic errors globally. (By feeding them to MegaReplacer.)

   c. Fact-check anything that makes you feel twitchy. (The Internet is your friend here. Using a search engine is like having a prosthetic memory.)

   d. Enter queries in the form the client prefers—inline, Word Comment, footnote—remembering that there's plenty of room to be polite and attentive to the author's nerves, and that abbreviations and cryptic notes are best avoided entirely. (I use AutoCorrect or AutoText for things I find I ask or explain often.)

   e. Edit the figures on hard copy (if required); if not, insert notes describing any necessary changes in the text—either where the figure is first cited, in the figure caption, or in the art file. Check the art to be sure it supports the text and contains no contradictions to the text. (Note: You may find it useful to study the figures before reading the text. That often makes it easier to spot inconsistencies or superfluous repetition in the author's discussion.)

   f. Typemark or style headings, text, and other markup features as required. Macros are very useful for this step.

6. *Consolidate the list of citations and vet it against the references, querying as needed*, as described in chapter 1, steps 3 and 4.
7. *Check the table of contents against the chapter titles and query as needed.*

8. *Typemark the file openers.* I like to do this in one sitting, as the book-title running head is provided by a macro that gets updated from project to project.
9. *Make the second edit pass.* Read everything again and fix whatever needs fixing.
    a. Be alert for verbatim repetition. (For some reason, I rarely notice this on the first reading. Then, the second time through, a phrase will strike a chord—at which point a file search often reveals that the author has said something the same way twice—or more.)
    b. Check the revision marks to be sure they make sense.
10. *Clean up the files.*
    a. Convert the footnotes or endnotes from the embedded Word feature if necessary. (But it's often better to leave them alone until after the author reviews the manuscript.)
    b. Review the queries for sense and tone. Revise any that seem to score points off the author or to be unlikely to get a clear, unambiguous response. ("Yes" or "OK" is the best answer.)
    c. Check the spelling—with a dictionary at hand!
    d. Add new words from the spelling check to the style sheet.
11. *Finish the style sheet.*
    a. Sort each section and remove duplicate entries.
    b. Check out any conflicts and correct the files as needed.
    c. Add the completion date.
12. *Prepare the cover letter and invoice, close up the job, and send it off.*

This process assumes that the files will return to me after the author reviews them, and I will then resolve the queries and clear the tracking. If I'm not going to see the files again, in step 10 I will also check the typemarking and make sure italics and boldface are applied to adjacent punctuation and spaces (or left off them) as the client requires.

Oh—and one more step: Calculate the pages-per-hour throughput on the job and the effective hourly rate it paid, and spend a few minutes thinking about what happened and what could have been further automated so as to go faster with the same or improved quality. On screen, there's always a better way....

Index

Page numbers in *italics* refer to figures and tables.

N

O

P

Q

R

S

T

U

V

About the Author

Hilary Powers has been freelancing since mid-1994 when she settled on editing as the skill most likely to allow her to emulate Nero Wolfe and avoid leaving home on business. She started working on screen before the end of that year, and abandoned paper entirely after only four projects. Now, around six hundred projects later, she still learns some new trick or shortcut on almost every job.

Editing is her fourth career. She settled into it happily for the long term, after working as a government analyst, an internal auditor and computer security specialist, and a nonprofit manager. For more info, see her website at http://www.powersedit.com.

These days, however, editing has to fight a new passion for her attention. See http://www.salamanderfeltworks.com for where wool-gathering and imagination are taking her....

OTHER EFA PUBLICATIONS AND RESOURCES

The EFA has a variety of resources available on topics of interest to editorial freelancers.

Books and booklets published by the EFA cover subjects such as electronic editing, résumé preparation, grammar, copyright and permissions, indexing, book production, textbook development, social media, and organization of a freelance business. For a current list of all titles and ordering information, visit the website at http://www.the-efa.org/res/booklets.php.

The EFA website, http://www.the-efa.org, offers a number of online resources. Popular are the "Code of Fair Practice," which defines ethical standards and contract guidelines for editorial freelancers and clients; the "Editorial Rates" table; a list of online reference sources such as specialized websites and dictionaries; and an archive of articles from the Freelance Editorial Association News, the official publication of the now-defunct Freelance Editorial Association.

The EFA newsletter, The Freelancer, features articles on freelance and communication issues, book and software reviews, columns on taxes and language usage, reports on EFA meetings and activities, letters from readers, and more. Published bimonthly, it is a complimentary benefit of EFA membership.

CPSIA information can be obtained
at www.ICGtesting.com
Printed in the USA
LVHW042001280323
742726LV00018B/1297

9 781880 407325